FDIC DIRECTOR SUITS: LESSONS LEARNED

AMERICAN ASSOCIATION OF BANK DIRECTORS

DAVID BARIS
Executive Director
American Association of Bank Directors

JARED KELLY
American Association of Bank Directors

FDIC Director Suits: Lessons Learned

2012 Edition

Copyright ©

American Association of Bank Directors
National Capital Office
1250 24th Street, NW, Suite 700
Washington, DC 20037

www.AABD.org

ISBN-13: 978-1480216556

ISBN-10: 1480216550

WHAT BANK DIRECTORS CAN LEARN FROM FDIC SUITS AGAINST DIRECTORS OF FAILED BANKS

TABLE OF CONTENTS

APPENDICES

INTRODUCTION AND SUMMARY

The American Association of Bank Directors has undertaken a review of the FDIC's civil suits against directors of failed banks and savings institutions to find out what directors of open banks can learn from the thirty-four complaints (involving more than 250 directors) filed from July 2010 through October 29, 2012.[1]

We undertook this study primarily to assist AABD members and others who currently serve as bank directors in helping to avoid the fate of those who have been sued.[2] Studies on the causes of bank failures and what can be learned from them are plentiful for the failures of banks and savings and loans during the S&L crisis of the late 1980's and early 1990's, but not for the more recent failures. A bibliography of many of the earlier studies and a few more recent studies is provided in Appendix I in addition to more recent studies.

Many of the complaints are not drafted in a way that provides clear guidance to those who wish to learn from them. Some make assertions that require bank directors to be clairvoyant, all-knowing or all-powerful in fixing or avoiding problems – clearly skill sets not required for bank directors to meet their fiduciary duties. There is no guidance AABD can provide that would help bank directors become clairvoyant or control events outside their control or never to make a mistake in judgment.

---

[1] The FDIC has authorized additional suits against 77 failed institutions and 647 individual defendants. Federal Deposit Insurance Corporation, *Professional Liability Lawsuits, available at* http://www.fdic.gov/bank/individual/failed/pls/ (last visited Sept. 23, 2012). 447 financial institutions have failed since August 2008. Federal Deposit Insurance Corporation, *Failed Bank List*, http://www.fdic.gov/bank/individual/failed/banklist.html (last visited Sept. 23, 2012).

[2] For comparison, nearly 25% of the total failed institutions during the Savings and Loan crisis resulted in lawsuits, while only 32 suits have been filed out of the 447 bank failures, or about 7%. However, if the additional 77 lawsuits that have been authorized are combined with the 32 filed suits, the percentage is also roughly 25% (109 out of 447).

7

One major finding in this Report is that bank directors are at higher risk of potential personal liability if they approve individual loans than if they do not. Almost all of the complaints assert that directors, as members of the Board of Directors or a director loan committee, approved loans on which their bank suffered losses, and that the loans should not have been made. The complaints suggest that bank directors who approve loans are held to the standard of a professional lending officer or credit officer. If there is a flaw in the loan analysis or in the appraisal or a "red flag" that the board or board committee should have inquired about but didn't, the complaints suggest that the director is legally responsible for the losses on the loan.

As a consequence, the Report recommends that bank directors, as board or board committee members, stop approving individual loans other than those required by law to be approved by a board or board committee. At the federal level, only loans subject to Regulation O are required to be approved by a bank board of directors.

AABD has previously requested that the FDIC approve a "safe harbor" for directors on boards or board committees that approve or ratify loans, but the FDIC has refused. The FDIC also disagrees with AABD's advice to bank directors not to approve individual loans because the FDIC believes that bank directors of community banks who know the community and the people who reside or do business there can add value by reviewing and approving loans. AABD agrees that community bank directors can add value, but not at the price of elevating potential personal liability. Once the FDIC approves a safe harbor for directors who act in good faith and without personal conflict in approving individual loans, AABD will withdraw its recommendation. See Appendices III and IV for AABD's correspondence with the FDIC.

Even if bank directors do not approve loans, they are still susceptible to potential lawsuits if their bank fails. This Report will summarize the other bases that the FDIC has used to sue directors of failed banks and recommendations on how directors might minimize potential liability and risk of suit by the FDIC.

The FDIC complaints make allegations against outside directors that implicitly require board members to have skills that many do not currently possess. While the federal banking agencies do not require bank directors to have specific training or background prior to assuming their positions or require any ongoing training, AABD believes that bank directors need to do so in order to mitigate risks of personal liability. Such training is not a requirement to meet fiduciary duties but may provide additional skills to bank directors to avoid actions by their banks that might later be used as a basis of personal liability.

AABD provides the tools by which bank directors can become better prepared to mitigate personal liability risks and become more valuable board members over matters that they can control. Among the resources offered to AABD members is a six-hour core course specially designed for outside board members conducted on bank premises or other location designated by the board of directors. Details of the core course and AABD's bank director certificate program are available on its website at www.aabd.org. AABD also offers independent assessments of bank boards of directors that provide recommendations on how to minimize personal liability risks and improve board and board committee governance.

We have considered the 1992 FDIC Statement on the Duties and Responsibilities of Bank Directors and Officers ("1992 FDIC Statement" or "Statement"). Although the 1992 FDIC Statement, in our view, is outdated and woefully inadequate, the FDIC continues to rely heavily on it to help decide whether to approve and file civil suits against directors and officers of failed banks. In that light, it is essential for current bank directors to familiarize themselves with the language in the 1992 FDIC Statement and attempt to conduct their business in a manner that will be consistent with the standards set forth in the 1992 FDIC Statement. See Appendix II for a copy of the FDIC Statement.

In a separate report, the American Association of Bank Directors explains what is wrong with the FDIC's Professional Liability Program as it is applied to former directors of closed institutions. This Report is not a critique of that program, but rather is an effort to assist current directors in minimizing potential personal liability and the risk of being sued in case their bank ever fails.

In a related report, AABD summarizes the standards of care applicable to bank directors in all fifty states, the Business Judgment Rule applicable in each state, and the authority for bank directors to rely reasonably on the information and opinions of bank management, outside advisors, and board committees in making decisions.

The following section is a summary of the most common elements found in the FDIC's complaints. AABD then summarizes the provisions of the 1992 FDIC Statement pertaining to bank directors, followed by a set of recommendations to directors of open banks and savings institutions designed to avoid or minimize personal liability that can grow out these suits. These recommendations should not be interpreted as requirements for bank directors to meet their fiduciary duties. Finally, this Report summarizes each of the thirty-four suits filed against directors of failed banks and savings institutions since July 2010 (through October 29, 2012).

COMMON ALLEGATIONS IN FDIC COMPLAINTS

The following is a summary of the most common allegations identified in the FDIC complaints. It should be noted that all but two of the lawsuits filed to date have been brought against community bank directors. Only Washington Mutual and IndyMac were large institutions and only director-officers were sued in those two cases.

Loan Underwriting Policies and Procedures

One of the most commonly cited allegations in the complaints was the lack of proper oversight and adequate policies regarding the loan underwriting process. Specifically, missing documentation of borrower income and credit worthiness was used to support a negligent theory of liability. Collateral valuation was another issue cited in most of the complaints where collateral was purportedly overvalued, not appraised until after the loans were funded, or was not sufficient to cover the loan amounts dispersed. There were many issues with perfecting security interests in collateral because policies did not require staff to submit perfected security agreements at closing. High loan-to-value ratios were very commonly cited as an inherent problem with lending practices. These claims were made against inside and outside directors equally. Most of the claims related to the loss loans that individual directors personally approved.

Most of the complaints assume that directors who approved loans as members of the board or a board committee should have independently investigated loans presented by management for board approval to make certain the loans are underwritten properly, as if they were loan officers themselves and had no loan or credit officers who had reviewed the loans prior to the submission of the loans to the board or board committee.[3]

---

[3] The complaints typically cite deficiencies in the loan underwriting, credit administration, loan policies or in compliance with such policies, violations of law or regulation or violations of safe and sound lending practices for which the board member is held accountable even though the work in preparing the

Most of the complaints cited deficient loan administration and underwriting practices (e.g., using interest reserves for problem loans, poor appraisal practices, or not having updated financial information and updated appraisals at the time of origination or renewal, modification or extension).

Loan Approvals by the Board of Directors and/or a Board Loan Committee

All of the complaints brought against directors list individual loans on which the failed bank suffered losses. These loans were either approved or ratified by the board of directors, or the loans were approved by the bank loan committee that consisted of officers and directors. Four (4) complaints did not list any outside directors and were brought either against officers or director-officers only.

Ninety percent of the complaints were filed against directors who approved or ratified individual loans that suffered losses; the strong impression is left that board members who did not approve or ratify individual loans were generally not sued or were at a much lower risk of being sued. Note, however, that directors who were not present during approvals of loss loans or who abstained from votes on particular loss loans were sometimes named in complaints.

Ratification is an after-the-fact affirmation as to the approval of an individual loan. By the time the ratification is made, the Bank has a legal obligation to make the loan and in most cases has already funded the loan. But our reading of the FDIC complaints suggests that the FDIC makes no distinction between approval and ratification as to the potential liability of a bank director.

Most of the complaints asserted that the bank and its board or board loan committee violated loan policies, procedures and

documentation and recommendations was done by professional lenders and credit officers.

12

regulations. If the board or board committee approved or ratified loans, the board or board committee members appear to be held to the same standard of knowledge and skills that would apply to a professional lender.

Lack of separation between the lending and credit function

Many loans were analyzed by the same loan officers who originated the loans; in other words, there was a lack of separation between the loan origination function and the credit underwriting and administration function. This led to a lack of internal quality control to make independent assessments regarding the safety of loans. In some complaints, the credit officer was deemed to lack independence because he or she reported to the Chief Lending Officer or Chief Executive Officer who had lending authority.

Approximately 75% of the complaints asserted that there was a lack of sufficient independence of the credit from the lending origination function.

Concentration of ADC or CRE Loans and Loans to Small Groups of Borrowers

Another common element cited in the complaints was the concentration of loans in either a small group of borrowers, in a specific geographic area, or a high concentration of ADC and CRE loans. In roughly a quarter of the complaints, the FDIC cited bank concentration of loans to a small pool of borrowers. For example, one bank had a group of 10 large borrowers that represented nearly 100% of bank capital to loan ratio. In all but two complaints, the concentration of ADC and CRE loans was cited as dangerously high. This concentration was always compared to peer groups and the concentrations cited in bank regulatory guidance. In all the complaints that listed ADC and CRE loan concentrations as a problem, the percentage of ADC/CRE loans to capital was substantially more than the peer group average or the regulatory guidance limit recommended (often ADC/CRE loans were well over 700% of the bank's capital before the bank's closing).

13

Many of the complaints cited continuing ADC/CRE lending in late 2006 and later in face of national, regional and local real estate markets weakening.

All but one of the complaints cited insufficient risk management systems to address loan concentrations.

Offering a new financial product or entering new geographic markets

A small number of the complaints cited the board's failure to properly plan for the offering of new financial products or entering new geographic markets. The FDIC claimed that the failed banks took excessive risks without implementing protections or hiring experienced employees. Finally, about a third of the complaints took issue with the concentration of loans in certain local geographic areas known to be experiencing a real estate market decline. At the same time, some complaints noted the making of loans outside the bank's core area as an issue because of the lack of familiarity with economic trends outside the bank's immediate vicinity.

Incompetent or inexperienced management

Approximately 55% of the complaints state that the directors did not ensure that the bank had competent and sufficient personnel in place to engage in the lending activities in which the bank was engaged.

Excessive growth strategies during challenging economy

About half the complaints asserted that boards created strategies that encouraged growth rates and excessive loan originations. The FDIC often cited stated goals that included boards acknowledging financial problems but deciding to attempt to "grow out" of the issues. Most banks wanted to gain market share and did so by encouraging rapid growth in generating high-risk loans, either in the ADC/CRE sector or through the use of "creative" financing agreements such as adjustable rate or subprime mortgages. Moreover, the incentives sometimes created by rewarding loan officers for generating these loans compounded the problems because it led to more high-risk loans.

Approximately 60% criticized board members for permitting the bank to grow rapidly, in many cases based on the use of non-core liabilities and brokered deposits.

Approximately 80% of the complaints asserted that board members failed to follow economic conditions either at all or not sufficiently, and didn't document those efforts or change the bank's lending as a result.

About 20% claimed board members should have known as early as August 2006 that continued underwriting of ADC/CRE loans was imprudent because the market was overheated.

Compensation systems that incentivize the taking of unreasonable risk

Some complaints alleged conflicts of interest in the bank's compensation structures because loan officers were awarded for originating new loans whether or not the loans were high quality. Most of the time, loan officers' compensation were not adversely affected by having originated loans on which the bank suffered losses. The compensation systems were usually cited as exacerbating the problems of irresponsible and excessive growth strategies.

Approximately 40% claimed that incentive compensation rewarded loan officers for volume without consideration of the quality of loans.

Insider loans and illegal or imprudent use of bank funds

In about a quarter of the complaints, the FDIC cited the board's approval of either illegal or fiscally imprudent use of bank funds to support a breach of fiduciary duty claim. For example, in one complaint the bank authorized dividend payments based on false profitability numbers created by using interest reserves to show profits. In another, the bank paid dividends to its holding company when under state law it was illegal to do so. Further, loans made to directors or officers were cited by the FDIC. One bank gave preferential treatment to a group of board members who used the funds in a failed business venture. Finally, the use of bank funds for personal expenses was noted in at least two complaints as a breach of fiduciary duty. For example, a donation was made to an event that was the wedding of a board member. Excessive use of funds for director meetings in exotic and luxurious locations was cited as wasteful spending.

Directors ignored or refused to follow regulators' suggestions and warnings

Virtually all of the FDIC complaints assert that banking agencies issued warnings and suggestions in multiple reports of examination that were ultimately not heeded. The most common warnings were the high concentration of ADC/CRE loans, improper underwriting policies, lack of internal controls and oversight over lending, use of brokered deposits, and improper use of interest reserves to support loan financing. The complaints use the lack of effective action in response to these warnings that put the board on notice as creating a gross negligence theory of liability. The argument was that because the directors knew that their policies were adverse to safe and conservative growth strategy and sound underwriting procedures, the boards and officers acted recklessly.

Standard of care asserted in complaints

In most cases, the FDIC complaints assert claims for both simple and gross negligence. In addition, they generally assert breach of fiduciary duties without specifying whether the breach is based on simple or gross negligence.

As explained in the next section, the U.S. Supreme Court decided in 1995 that the FDIC's claim that there was a simple negligence standard applicable to bank directors was wrong. Instead, the Court ruled that a federal statute applies a gross negligence standard as defined by state law unless the state has a more stringent standard (simple negligence), in which case the FDIC may sue on that standard.

As previously mentioned, AABD has issued a report on the standard of care in each of the fifty states. Our reading suggests that the vast majority of the states have adopted a gross negligence standard of care, whether directly through statutory provisions, or through courts applying the Business Judgment Rule. Nevertheless, the FDIC complaints in states where a gross negligence standard has been adopted often include a simple negligence claim.

THE 1992 FDIC STATEMENT

The 1992 FDIC Statement sets forth its expectations of outside directors and the standards by which it evaluates whether to sue outside directors.

The FDIC states that directors are responsible for the following:

- Selecting, monitoring, and evaluating competent management;
- Establishing business strategies and policies;
- Monitoring and assessing the progress of business operations;
- Establishing and monitoring adherence to policies and procedures required by statute, regulation, and principles of safety and soundness; and
- Making business decisions on the basis of fully informed and meaningful deliberation

According to the 1992 FDIC Statement, directors must require timely and ample information to discharge board responsibilities. Directors are also responsible for requiring management to respond promptly to supervisory criticism.

The FDIC states that it "will not bring civil suits against directors . . . who fulfill their responsibilities, including the duties of loyalty and care, and who make reasonable business judgments on a fully informed and after proper deliberation."

The 1992 FDIC Statement also summarizes the nature of the suits filed by the FDIC against directors, which includes cases:

- where the director engaged in dishonest conduct or approved or condoned abusive transactions with insiders;
- where a director was responsible for the failure of an institution to adhere to applicable laws and regulations, its own policies, or any agreement with a supervisory

authority or where the director otherwise participated in a safety or soundness violation; or

- where directors failed to establish proper underwriting policies and to monitor adherence thereto, or approved loans that they knew or had reason to know were improperly underwritten, or where the board failed to heed warnings from regulators or professional advisors

The 1992 FDIC Statement recognizes that one of the factors considered in determining whether to bring an action against a director is the distinction between inside and outside directors. Outside directors generally do not participate in the conduct of the day-to-day business operations of the bank. The most common suits brought against outside directors, according to the Statement, either involve insider abuse or situations where the director failed to heed warnings from regulators, accountants, attorneys or others that there was a significant problem in the bank which required correction.

Although the Statement recognizes the distinction between outside and inside directors and between outside directors and management, it is not entirely consistent in that distinction. For example, it identifies lawsuits related to directors approving loans that they knew or had reason to know were improperly underwritten. But when boards and board committees do approve loans (and many community bank boards and board loan committees do so even though not required to do so), they typically are not supplanting the loan and credit officers who previously reviewed the loans in depth and recommended approval, or the officer loan committee that might have recommended approval, but rather their review is a high level review of whether the loan should be made consistent with the overall strategy of the bank.

The Statement also fails to acknowledge the Business Judgment Rule, which in many states means that the board members are protected from personal liability if they exercised their business judgment in good faith and without a conflict of interest. Nor does it recognize that directors may reasonably rely on the work of officers and employees, advisors, and board committees in reaching decisions such as whether to approve a loan, set policy and risk tolerances, and adopt internal controls and systems.

FDIC used to believe that the applicable standard of care for bank directors was simple negligence based on federal common law. However, the U.S. Supreme Court ruled in the mid-1990's that the FDIC and RTC were incorrect; the standard of care is gross negligence unless the law of the state where the failed institution was based has a more stringent standard.

In its 1997 Annual Report, the FDIC stated that regardless of state law, it will not sue a director unless the director committed gross negligence, although the FDIC will assert a simple negligence count in suits involving failed banks in states that have a simple negligence standard. Because this policy was adopted following the adoption of the 1992 FDIC Statement, it is not reflected in that statement.

The 1992 FDIC Statement states that directors need to be "fully informed" prior to making decisions or else they might be in breach of their fiduciary duties. This is not an accurate statement of the law in most, if not all jurisdictions. Directors should be sufficiently informed of material facts or reasonably rely on others to enable them to make a reasonable decision, but to be "fully" informed is an ideal that is seldom realized and should not be a standard by which the FDIC should attempt to assess personal liability. AABD does not believe that it is possible for bank directors to be "fully informed", certainly not in the literal sense.

The Statement refers to a requirement to make "reasonable" decisions based on "proper deliberation." This, too has a subjective context to it – what does that really mean? The Statement does not explain what is meant by proper deliberation. We address this issue in the Recommendations section of this Report.

The 1992 FDIC Statement highlights the importance of heeding the warnings of regulators and others and how not doing so can motivate the FDIC to file suit against directors.

The allegation that directors have not heeded the warnings of the banking agencies is a common one. These allegations frequently are stated in reports of examination, sometimes without much documentation or detail. Many seem to be based on the fact that the directors have not been able to successfully improve the financial condition of the institution or its loan quality or reduce concentrations. However, directors do not have total control over improving the financial condition of their institution. That depends to a great degree on the local economy. Similarly, matters such as being able to move a loan from substandard to pass, or obtaining all relevant updated financial information from a borrower who refuses to provide such information or obtaining additional collateral from an unwilling borrower are not within the power of the board to effectuate.

Failure to achieve improvement in loan quality or effectuate actions that require third party cooperation is fundamentally different from a refusal by a board of directors to do what is clearly within its power to do, such as amending a loan policy in accordance with the instructions of the examiners or adopting an ALLL methodology that the examiners instructed the bank to adopt. But our experience is that purposely flouting the authority of the banking agencies is highly unusual. Most boards of directors and management of banks want to satisfy the demands of the banking agencies particularly given the enormous power of the agencies to punish those who do not comply with their directives.

Notwithstanding the omissions and misstatements in this outdated Statement, directors of open banks need to take its content seriously. The FDIC has asserted on its website that it relies on the Statement to help it decide whether to sue a director of a failed bank. We will address how directors may attempt to meet the expectations of the FDIC in the Recommendations section of this Report.

RECOMMENDATIONS TO MITIGATE RISK OF PERSONAL LIABILITY

In light of the assertions made in the FDIC complaints, and based on a reading of the 1992 FDIC Statement, AABD has the following recommendations to directors of open banks:

Consider resigning.

If a director is dissatisfied with the way in which a bank is being supervised or managed and believes that this will not change, then our advice is to resign. Resignation does not protect a director from liability for actions taken prior to the resignation.

Don't let your bank fail.

The FDIC does not sue civilly as receiver unless the bank has failed. One way for a bank director to minimize personal liability risk is to avoid a bank failure. The recommendations in this Report, if followed, will also help minimize the risk of bank failure. While bank failures in the future may not fail for the same reasons as those that failed over the past few years, it is instructive to know that most of the banks that have failed since 2009 had three characteristics in common: 1) high concentrations in CRE/ADC lending; 2) fast growth; and 3) noncore deposits and nondeposit borrowings funding that growth.

Have the knowledge necessary to meet the fiduciary duties of a bank director.

The FDIC complaints make allegations of certain director failings that would not be overcome without thorough self-education or formal training. None of the federal banking agencies require a prequalifying test or course prior to a person becoming a bank director, nor do they require any ongoing training unless imposed through an enforcement action. It is up to the person and the bank on whose board he or she will serve to decide what knowledge and skills are necessary for the person to serve effectively and in a manner that will minimize the risk of personal liability. AABD offers a core course specially designed for an outside bank director whether the director has experience serving as a bank director or not. The AABD core course covers all of the subjects that directors need to have a grasp of in order to meet the standards (we believe standards that are higher than is required by the duty of care and duty of loyalty) implicit in the FDIC complaints.

Adopt strong indemnification provisions in the articles and bylaws of both the bank and its parent company.

Depending on applicable state law, the board of directors should take action to assure that language is in the articles of incorporation or bylaws of the bank and its parent company that provides the broadest indemnification for directors as possible under state law. It is surprising how many banks do not have this language in their articles of bylaws. In addition, some banks will take the additional step of entering into indemnification agreements with their directors. If a bank fails, its indemnification of directors will have no value, but if a parent company survives, it can indemnify directors of the bank if the indemnification provisions have been properly drafted.

Retain a knowledgeable D&O insurance agent and confirm that the coverage for liability against regulatory actions is adequate.

Too frequently in our experience, banks have bought D&O insurance that the Board thought covered them adequately against bank regulatory risk, only to find out later that the risk was not covered adequately or at all. It is essential that a bank's insurance agent be experienced and well-versed in D&O insurance policies and have access to a number of different carriers who specialize in D&O policies for banks and their directors. Having an attorney knowledgeable in this coverage and policy language also can be very helpful.

Think and act defensively and with a degree with paranoia.

Once a bank fails, it can take three years and sometimes longer for the FDIC to file a suit against directors. During that period, the FDIC staff and outside counsel will pore over bank documents searching for information that would give them grounds to sue directors and officers. Board and Board committee minutes, loan files, and other corporate documents will be scrutinized. The deliberative process of the board and its committees will be evaluated. When a board or board committee makes a decision, they should consider the possibility that another set of eyes many years from the time of the decision will be reviewing how the decision was documented for an entirely different purpose.

Do not approve loans at the Board of Director or Board Committee level.

The FDIC complaints treat bank directors who voted in favor of approving loans at board or board committee meetings as if they are loan or credit officers. AABD does not believe that most directors are willing to do that, and recommends that directors not play that role. See Appendix IV for additional material on this issue.

If the Board or Board Committee continues to approve loans, extraordinary steps need to be taken to protect against personal liability, including thorough documentation of board and board committee decisions.

In a separate report, AABD will provide practical guidance on what steps a board or board committee can take to mitigate the risks of personal liability when approving loans. These will include having a written loan policy specifically limiting the role of the board or board committee in approving loans (that is, making it clear that they are not conducting a de novo review, but are relying reasonably on the work and recommendations of the lending and credit staff) and requiring loan and credit officers to make certain written representations with the presentation to the board or board committee. In addition, the loan policy should permit any exceptions to policy if approved by the board or board committee. Loan packages going to the board need to have sufficient information for the board to make an informed decision or where information is lacking, obtaining written confirmation that the appropriate loan or credit officer reviewed that information and was satisfied that the information was sufficient to support the approval of the loan. Every conceivable "red flag", including any variance from the loan policy or from agency directives or guidance, should be vetted and documented as to how the board or board addressed the red flag, including any direction that the board or committee provided to bank management. If discussion of the loans includes discussions outside the board or board committee meetings (such as between meetings through emails and telephone calls), those discussions should be memorialized by reference to them during the official meetings and have the minutes reflect those discussions. Careful review of board and board committee minutes prior to approval by the board or board committee is also essential.

Maintain a separate, independent credit function from the lending origination function.

The credit officer must be separate from the lending officers and must report to the board, a board committee or to the CEO but only if the CEO is not a loan officer or have authority to approve loans as if he or she were a loan officer. The credit officer cannot be compensated based on the volume of loans booked.

Pay special attention to loan concentrations.

Before a bank decides to have loan concentrations, the board should review the benefits and risks to such concentrations, and what risk management processes need to be in place and the management resources necessary to reasonably control such risks.[4]

Document the decisions to hire and retain competent senior loan and credit officers.

Most bank failures are a result of loans going bad. The Board or a board committee need not ordinarily be involved in the hiring of junior loan or credit officers and other lending staff members, but should be involved in the hiring, firing, and assessments for the senior loan and senior credit officer. If the bank is entering a new lending category or moving into a new geographic market or creating or expanding a loan concentration, the board or board committee should be involved in the process of evaluating whether the bank has the appropriate personnel in place for such change.

Adopt, direct implementation of, and oversee a rigorous risk management system.

The FDIC complaints often make reference to deficient risk management practices. Boards and board committees should review the bank regulatory guidance on risk management to assure that they are meeting the current expectations of their banking regulators. Loan concentrations in particular require enhanced risk management systems and, in some cases, additional capital.

Assure that Board reports and packages and board minutes reflect that business judgment is informed and exercised reasonably.

---

[4] *See* Federal Deposit Insurance Corporation, *Managing Commercial Real Estate Concentrations, available at* http://www.fdic.gov/regulations/examinations/supervisory/insights/siwin07/artic le02_real_estate.html (last visited Sept. 26, 2012); Office of the Comptroller of the Currency, OCC Bulletin 2006-46, *Interagency Guidance on CRE Concentration Risk Management, available at* http://www.occ.treas.gov/news-issuances/bulletins/2006/bulletin-2006-46.html (last visited Sept. 26, 2012).

Decisions by boards and board committees, particularly major decisions (strategic decisions, material changes in the loan or investment portfolio, material changes in management, and approval of loans and large investments) need to be supported by the record available to the board or board committee at the time the decision was made. Many decisions involve a balancing of risk and reward, pros and cons. It's a good idea for the record to reflect that the board or board committee considered all of the factors, good and bad, in reaching its decision. Review of board and committee minutes before they are adopted or accepted should be carefully done to be sure that they are accurate and reflect the deliberate and prudent oversight of the board or board committee. When discussions among board members and management are held outside a board or board committee meeting that bears on the decisions being made, it is advisable that those discussions be documented during a board or board committee meeting so that the record will be clear that those discussions formed a part of the decision-making process.

Anticipate problems early through use of red flags, and take prompt corrective action once the problems are identified.

Virtually every bank, like any other business, will suffer reverses and face challenges. The banks that survive these challenges often are the ones that discover the problem early, and then take effective and timely corrective action. The identification of red flags as an early warning system is important.[5]

Establish a prudent written loan policy, an independent credit function, qualified third party loan review, and a system of checks and balances to assure effective Board monitoring over the lending function.

---

[5] *See* Office of the Comptroller of the Currency, *Detecting Red Flags in Board Reports: A Guide for Directors, available at* http://www.occ.gov/publications/publications-by-type/other-publications-reports/rf_book.pdf (last visited Sept. 26, 2012).

Whether or not the board of directors or a board committee approves loans, the board is expected to establish a prudent written loan policy. This policy should be reviewed at least annually by management and the board. To help defend a board's decision to approve or amend a loan policy, it is helpful to have a qualified third party review and recommend changes in the loan policy prior to adoption. To help assure that individual loans are being made consistent with the requirements of the loan policy and underwriting standards, the board should direct management to establish an independent credit function headed by an experienced and qualified individual. A qualified third party loan review is also very helpful in provide the board with a means to monitor the loan process and loan quality. A system of checks and balances involves a series of steps and processes that the Board establishes and monitors that will allow the board to monitor compliance with the loan policy and the quality of the loan portfolio; trends in the loans and loan quality, adequacy of the loan and credit personnel; and identification and resolution of risk in the loan portfolio and future lending.

Respond in writing to any and all criticisms in reports of examination, correspondence from banking agencies, and audit reports, and direct that corrective action be taken and verify that it has been taken.

Boards of directors typically rely heavily on management to respond to reports of examination. But the FDIC complaints suggest that it may be necessary for Boards to take a more active role in responses. If there is disagreement with comments or conclusions in the reports of examination, it is essential that the bank respond in writing explaining why it disagrees. Where corrective action is required, the Bank needs to respond in writing in a very detailed and precise way on the corrective action being taken and to request a prompt response from the bank regulator that the proposed corrective action is acceptable. The role of the Board is to ask for a full briefing on the results of the report of examination, where there is disagreement, and the corrective action that is being proposed – before the response is finalized. If the board's questioning results in a disagreement with management, that disagreement needs to be worked out prior to the preparation of the final response to the banking agency. The board should also ask for updates from management as to what corrective action was taken and when it was taken, and management's corrective action should be memorialized in the minutes of the board or board committee meeting or attached to the minutes.

Take adequate steps to support the bank's efforts to comply with a formal or informal administrative action.

Boards should evaluate the adequacy of bank resources to assure that the bank will be able to comply with the terms of a formal or informal administrative action. The Board role should also include careful monitoring of compliance and approval of actions required of it by the document. Use of a qualified third party such as a retired examiner to assist in the compliance effort can help the bank do a better job and also help protect the board from later criticism.

Do not pay incentive compensation that will encourage unacceptable risks.

In community banks, this issue most commonly arises in the context of paying bonuses to loan officers based on the volume of loans originated. Boards should require that incentive compensation to loan officers be also dependent on the quality of the loans being booked and the experience with such loans after booking. Some banks are beginning to use clawback provisions that will allow the bank to seek repayment of bonuses by the loan officer if the performance of the loan portfolio is unacceptable. There is bank regulatory guidance on this subject and regulations required by Dodd-Frank will be issued in the near future.[6]

---

[6] Guidelines and proposed regulations can be found in OCC Bulletin 2010-24 at: www.occ.gov/news-issuances/bulletins/2010/bulletin-2010-24.html (last visited Sept. 26, 2012). For proposed regulations see SEC proposed rules for incentive compensation at financial institutions: www.sec.gov/news/press/2011/2011-57.htm (last visited Sept. 26, 2012).

Avoid insider transactions that cannot be fully justified as arms length and nonpreferential.

Some boards of directors will decide that it is more prudent to decide to have no insider transactions. If insider transactions do occur, the insider whose interests are affected must disclose the conflict or apparent conflict in writing and not participate in any way in the review and approval of the transaction.

Conduct a review of policies, procedures, corporate documents and corporate governance to determine personal liability risk and how to mitigate it.

AABD now offers reviews of a bank's policies, procedures, corporate documents and corporate governance to determine what changes the Board can adopt that can mitigate its members' personal liability risk.

Assume that a simple negligence standard applies to your board members even if your bank is not based in a simple negligence state.

Bank directors should assume that the FDIC will make every effort to assert a claim based on simple negligence if their bank fails. Therefore, boards of directors and board committees should conduct themselves in a manner that will avoid any allegation of simple negligence.

Periodic evaluation of the local, state, regional and national economy.

The FDIC complaints frequently assert that the Board of Directors of the failed bank did not take the downturn into account and continued to make CRE and ADC loans in declining markets or ones that could have been foreseen as declining. Boards of Directors should reflect in their minutes discussions about the economy and how changes or anticipated changes might affect the bank's business and risks, and whether any changes in the bank's business or how it conducts business are warranted. The board of directors should be provided with sufficient information in order to reach an informed decision as to what steps, if any, should be taken in response to the changes. Once the board of directors has the information, it should be within its reasonable business judgment to decide how the bank should react, if at all, to such changes even if it turns out that the board made the wrong judgment. Changes in the economy and economic outlook could lead to changes in loan and investment underwriting standards, loan and investment type, concentrations, valuations, and other business of the Bank, including existing loans and investments.

THE FDIC COMPLAINTS

FDIC as Receiver for 1st Centennial Bank v. Appleton, et al.
Filed January 14, 2011 in the U.S. District Court for the
Central District of California

The complaint was filed against officers, inside directors, and outside directors. Most of the directors also served on board loan committees and approved the specific loss loans cited by the FDIC. The claim alleged counts of negligence, gross negligence and breach of fiduciary duties. The complaint claimed simple negligence despite the gross negligence requirement under California law, established in the *Castetter* case in 1995. The FDIC claimed $26.8 million from the loss loans (out of a total of $163 million in losses to the DIF) and sought to recover $26.8 million from the defendants.

Bank had a high concentration of CRE/ADC loans ranging from 35-43% of total loans, whereas the bank's peers were only at 9-16% for the period from 2003 to 2008. Approximately 2/3 of the ADC/CRE loans were concentrated in single family residential tract construction loans, specifically tract housing.

The FDIC stated the bank's ADC loan to capital percentage was far too high. The bank ranked in the upper 90th percentile among peer institutions in terms of ADC loan to capital percentage, having anywhere from a 300% to over 1200% ADC loan to capital ratio prior to closing. Regulatory guidance set the limit of ADC loans to capital at just 100% and managers were on notice of this requirement. *Guidance on Concentrations*, 71 Fed. Reg. 74580-01, 87 (2006).

The over-concentration was a result of the bank's strategy to grow exponentially in CRE lending over five years. Most loans were made in single family tracts within a very limited geographic area. FDIC examiners warned the bank as early as March 2004 that there were problematic loan concentrations, but the bank disregarded the warnings and the proposed strategies recommended by the FDIC.

The FDIC criticized the use of brokered deposits as opposed to core deposits.

The bank had weak internal controls over lending. The FDIC specifically pointed to the following weaknesses in CRE lending: failed to mitigate losses associated with increased CRE lending, inappropriately used interest reserves, inadequately monitored concentration growth from month to month, and did not categorize CRE loans by risk for simplified review processes.

The board violated bank policies regarding prudent banking standards in the following ways: allowed loan to value ratios to exceed 75%, relied on stale financial data and failed to conduct due diligence to ensure accurate market data, did not ensure accurate collateral valuation, made loans to borrowers without any cash down payments, did not update appraisals made for various loan increases, and did not place loans on non-accrual when payment was reasonably unlikely.

The directors recklessly failed to assess market conditions by not properly determining market supply and demand via thorough due diligence. The FDIC claimed the bank should have monitored population changes, zoning requirements, rental rates and sales prices, new construction and absorption rates, and valuation trends for discount and direct capitalization rates. The FDIC asserted there was clear indication the California real estate market was declining.

The FDIC cited incompetent managers and negligent supervision issues. The bank should have ensured that compensation structures did not create conflicts of interest or perverse incentives for employees. One Vice President (Construction Lending) was in charge of too many areas (e.g., originating loans, ensuring sound underwriting, overseeing the appraisal process, and ensuring loan applications were high quality), which created a conflict of interest. The incentive compensation plan further aggravated the conflicts because that single VP could achieve over 100% of his base salary by approving a greater amount of loans. The structure encouraged strategies that disregarded loan quality in favor of loan quantity.

Outside directors were also cited for negligent oversight of managerial decisions leading to aggressive, risky lending. The complaint claims it is the responsibility of directors to ensure the careful, reasonable, prudent and non-negligent underwriting and administration of 1st Centennial's; to ensure that 1st Centennial did not engage in unsafe, unsound, unreasonable and imprudent practices; to ensure that competent management carries out the policies of the bank; must ensure that neither the compensation structure nor job descriptions create any conflicts of interests.

The complaint stated the Board "should have stopped new CRE lending by January 2007; it was a breach of the fiduciary duties . . . on the part of directors to allow 1st Centennial to be managed by officers incapable of managing the risk that the Bank's strategy . . . created."

The 2008 ROE was attached as an exhibit showing that as late as February 2007, the examiners considered the Bank as a CAMELS 2 bank, with a 1 management component rating.

FDIC as Receiver for Alpha Bank & Trust v. Blackwell, et al.
Filed October 7, 2011 in the U.S. District Court for the Northern District of Georgia

The complaint was brought against inside and outside directors; most all the outside directors were on the board loan committee that approved the loss loans. The complaint alleged simple and gross negligence against all defendants. The FDIC sought to recover $23.92 million in damages, the same amount of the aggregate losses attributed to the loss loans. The bank's failure led to an estimated loss of $214.5 million to the DIF. The bank had assets of roughly $354 million at the time of failure.

The FDIC claimed the bank created a compensation structure that awarded loan origination instead of loan performance. This led to risky ADC/CRE loans and exponential ADC/CRE loan to capital growth that was not supported by internal capital growth.

The bank financed risky loans with interest reserves. The FDIC claimed this practice was discouraged because it was reckless and negligent. Using interest reserves to finance ADC/CRE loans exposed the bank to an unreasonable amount of risk if the loans became delinquent or were written off.

The bank's strategy to relentlessly grow its loan portfolio caused the bank to ignore or reject regulators' suggestions to decrease the bank's high concentration in CRE loans. Regulators and third parties warned the defendants about the excessive concentration and underwriting issues.

ADC/CRE loans accounted for 78% of the bank's entire loan portfolio; this was contrary to the bank's own lending policy, which allowed only 40% of all loans to be in ADC/CRE loans. The FDIC alleged the bank disregarded its own loan policies and created unnecessary risk in doing so.

The FDIC pointed to incomplete or inadequate lending procedures and formal policies as a reason the bank ultimately stumbled. The bank failed to create proper policies regarding loan to value ratios, proper valuation standards, and prudent underwriting standards. The bank also failed to monitor and maintain proper capital to asset ratios. This failure allowed the bank to become highly leveraged.

The FDIC took issue with the lack of documentation the bank obtained on each loan it initiated. Common problems with documentation included: non-existent appraisals, inadequate or inaccurate financial information about borrowers' sources of income or security offered, and insufficient credit investigations. The FDIC claimed the defendants were responsible for overseeing this process and hiring competent employees to follow the bank's lending policy.

The FDIC claimed the defendants were aware, or should have been aware of the deficiencies in underwriting and loan support regarding the loss loans. Despite this knowledge, the defendants approved the loss loans. The FDIC used this fact to support a gross negligence claim.

FDIC as Receiver of Haven Trust Bank v. Briscoe, et al.
Filed July 14, 2011 in the U.S. District Court for the Northern District of Georgia

FDIC alleged simple and gross negligence and breach of fiduciary duty against officers, inside director-officers, and outside directors. Some of the directors were on the board loan committee while others were not. The FDIC sought to recover approximately $40 million, the precise amount caused by the loss loans. The bank's failure cost the deposit insurance fund roughly $248 million. The bank had assets of about $575 million when it failed.

The FDIC cited the following general concerns in the complaint: the bank failed to ensure adequate loan policies were in place; the bank failed to implement procedures and internal controls; the bank failed to adhere to existing loan policies, procedures and internal controls; the bank failed to ensure compliance with applicable laws and regulations; and the bank pursued a business model inconsistent with safe and sound banking practices.

The bank made multiple insider loans in violation of Regulation O and other regulations. This constituted a breach of the duty of loyalty. Directors received unsecured lines of credit and other preferential loan treatment for projects. The bank lost $7 million for one set of loans given to two directors who were attempting to form a separate business.

Collateral was a major issue cited by the FDIC. The agency alleged a number of issues with collateral including that the bank failed to inspect collateral or properly value the collateral. The FDIC claimed there were multiple items of real and personal property that were not properly perfected under state law (there was no attachment of a security interest, therefore, the collateral was subject to unsecured creditors and not subject to the secured credit protections the bank should have been granted). The FDIC noted that many appraisals were nonexistent or not properly undertaken. Various loans were under-secured as a result of the inadequate procedures.

The FDIC asserted the failure to heed regulatory warnings as a major issue facing the directors. Regulators issued multiple warnings that ADC loan concentrations and ADC capital to loan percentages were too high (around 400-600% ADC loans to capital). Capital to asset ratios were also cited as dangerously low, in the area of just 5-6% in 2008. CRE loan concentration was 58%, in violation of FDIC warnings as well as bank policy and procedures governing maximum concentrations. The FDIC claimed the defendants were on notice of these excessive concentrations.

Bank directors were cited for negligence because they were "responsible for analyzing loan applications and supporting documentation to ensure that loans were properly documented and otherwise satisfied the Bank's lending policies as well as prudent lending practices" and failed to do so adequately.
The FDIC claimed the directors were negligent because they did not satisfy their duties to select, monitor, and evaluate management; establish business strategies and policies; monitor and assess the bank's business operations; establish and monitor adherence to policies and procedures required by statute, regulation, and principles of safety and soundness; review and approve the actions of the loan committee; and make business decisions on the basis of fully informed and meaningful deliberation.

FDIC as Receiver of Heritage Community Bank v. Saphir, et al.
Filed November 1, 2010 in the U.S. District Court for the Northern District of Illinois

The FDIC complaint alleged claims of negligence, gross negligence, and breach of fiduciary duty. The defendants were inside directors or officers, and outside directors who sat on the board loan committee that approved loss loans relevant to the complaint. The loss loans resulted in $8.5 million in losses to the bank; the FDIC sued the directors for the precise amount and over $11 million in dividends that were paid. The bank had assets of approximately $232 million when it failed.

The FDIC cited a number of issues with the bank's CRE lending. The complaint alleges the board had no experience in CRE lending and consulted no managers or outside parties with experience on how to establish a CRE lending portfolio. The FDIC claims the bank began lending in this high risk area without experience and became overly aggressive in its loan growth.

The bank had issues with underwriting CRE loans. The bank conducted poor credit analyses of potential borrowers because they did not collect sufficient information or have a complete level of secondary review. Loan officers had the opportunity to rate their own loans and often inflated the ratings. Without the second level of review, there was no internal control over this practice.

The FDIC claimed that loan concentration and underwriting issues were complicated by awarding incentive pay for originating loans without assessing the quality of the loans. The complaint claims that by allowing a single manager to receive incentive compensation and complete credit analysis and underwriting functions, the board permitted unreasonable and irresponsible incentives.

The bank's CRE loans had excessive loan to value ratios. The FDIC claimed that CRE loan amounts were dangerously close to the estimated total future value of the collateral based on an "as completed" appraisal. The bank's loan policy provided that CRE loans should not exceed 80% of the expected future value of the property. The FDIC claimed the bank routinely exceeded these limits in making CRE loans. Defendants were allegedly liable for the approving these loans without conducting a reasonable amount of diligence regarding the loan concentrations.

Regulators suggested that the bank should have monitored the CRE loans more effectively to ensure the funds dispersed were in line with the project's completion. The bank never monitored and was unaware that some projects had stalled completely. When CRE loans began to fail, the bank's tracking procedures were non-existent.

The FDIC noted improper uses of interest reserves that led to unjustified dividends and profits. Income was not received from borrowers making loan payments in cash, rather it was recognized by merely increasing the outstanding balance of the CRE loan by drawing down on interest reserves provided for in the original loan and often increased by the bank once depleted. This created false profitability for the bank and was used to justify substantial dividends to investors in the bank's holding company and generous incentive compensation programs for senior management.

FDIC claimed the defendants should have caused the bank to cease new CRE lending, aggressively work out distressed loans, increase reserves, and strengthen bank capital after the real estate market began to fail in early 2007. Instead, defendants caused and allowed the bank to make new CRE loans and to extend and renew additional advances on non-performing loans to mask their problems.

FDIC as Receiver of Integrity Bank of Alpharetta, GA v. Skow, et al.
Filed January 14, 2011 in the U.S. District Court for the Northern District of Georgia

The FDIC brought counts of simple negligence, gross negligence, and breach of fiduciary duties against both inside director-officers and outside directors. Most directors were on the board loan committee that approved loans.. The simple negligence claims were dismissed by the federal judge on summary judgment; the gross negligence claims were retained for discovery. FDIC sought to recover $70 million in damages suffered from the loss loans. The bank had approximately $1.1 billion in assets when it failed. It cost the DIF an estimated $250 to $350 million.

The FDIC claimed the bank had no policies or procedures in place commensurate with the bank's extraordinary rate of growth and its risky lending strategy. The bank had one loan committee and it was only responsible for approving loans over $500,000. Only insider loans needed to be approved by the full board. The FDIC claimed this was inadequate oversight.

The FDIC claimed the bank was out of compliance with state banking regulations. The bank set its loan limit for individual borrowers to 35% of the bank's capital and surplus; Georgia only allowed a maximum loan limit for individual borrowers to 25% of capital and surplus.

Loan officers had control of both originating loans and ensuring loan quality. The FDIC claimed that this combination of responsibility created singular control over two important functions that should have been separated. Further, the combination created an even worse situation when coupled with the incentive based payments to loan officers for increasing loan volumes or generating new loans.

To attract CRE developers, the bank offered floating rate loans, interest only financing, and accepted security that contained only a small amount of equity. The collateral specifically was not sufficient to cover the loans and the loan-to-value ratio on the collateral was too high. The FDIC claimed this strategy was reckless and negligent because CRE and ADC loans were inherently risky and needed additional security to hedge against the risk.

The FDIC claimed that loan concentrations in risky loans products caused the bank to fail. ADC loan concentration dramatically increased from 2003-2007; beginning in 2005, the percentage of ADC concentration to bank capital increased from 386% to 931% without any significant increase in monitoring and reporting.

The bank failed to heed warnings from bank regulators regarding ADC loan concentration, the bank's rate of growth, and dangerously low capital levels. Regulators cited noncompliance with state banking regulations regarding loan limitations as irresponsible. The FDIC claimed the bank chose not to implement policies to remedy the problems. In fact, the bank increased lending to certain borrowers after they were warned to come into compliance. For example, one borrower was over 2.55 times the legal lending limit yet the bank granted a waiver of the limit to generate more loans.

The bank approved 15-20 loss loans to multiple parties that had issues with documentation, collateral valuation, inappropriate uses of interest reserves, and unexplainable disbursements of loan funds. These were the primary reasons the FDIC brought the action against the defendants.

FDIC as Receiver of Mutual Bank v. Mahajan, et al.
Filed October 25, 2011 in the U.S. District Court for the Northern District of Illinois

The FDIC alleged negligence, gross negligence, and breach of fiduciary duties. The defendants were inside and outside directors and officers, as well as the bank's attorney. The attorney was charged with negligence and legal malpractice. At least four defendants were close family members with the Chairman of the Board. The FDIC sought to recover $115 million from loss loans, $10.5 from unlawful dividends, and $1.09 million in wasted corporate assets. The bank failed with nearly $1.6 billion in assets. The bank's failure cost the DIF $696 million.

The FDIC cited a number of primary reasons for liability, including: the bank's reckless growth strategy focusing on ADC and CRE concentration; inadequate underwriting and credit administration practices; the bank ignored its own loan policies; the bank ignored federal lending regulations; and the bank disregarded regulators' warnings.

The FDIC made additional claims of corporate waste and improper dividend payments based on inflated company value. The directors approved $10.5 million in dividend payments that were deemed unlawful, facilitated payments for a director's wedding ($250,000) and the legal defense of a director's wife ($495,000), approved the usage of $300,000 for a director's meeting in Monte Carlo, and authorized $250,000 to pay excess amounts to contractors that were friends of directors.

ADC and CRE loan concentrations were more than three times the concentrations of peer banks. Further, concentration was focused in a small number of high volume borrowers, a concentration that exacerbates default risks. The FDIC claimed these policies were reckless and negligent.

The board failed to hire sufficient staff to support the extreme growth and concentrations into ADC and CRE lending. This resulted in many issues for the bank's documentation and loan approval procedures. The FDIC claimed many collateral appraisals were done after the loan was funded, loan guarantees were often missing from files, and loan terms were changed at closing without approval.

The FDIC alleged the bank had an extensive loan policy but failed to abide by the terms of the policy. The agency claimed this was reckless disregard and put the directors on notice that there were loan approval and documentation issues that needed to be addressed. The complaint claimed this was a failure to supervise.

The FDIC noted that regulators repeatedly warned the bank of various issues including loan concentration, improperly valued collateral, and capital requirements. One regulator warned the bank that risk management systems had not kept pace with the asset growth experienced.

The FDIC cited the bank's wasteful spending and facilitation of inappropriate payments for personal usages. This was a breach of the board's fiduciary duty of loyalty. As referenced above, the board authorized payments for individual and personal uses.

Under state law, the bank was not allowed to make any dividend payments because of its financial status as an institution not in good financial health. Yet, the bank made $10.5 million in dividend payments to its holding company, the stock of which was held almost exclusively by board members.

FDIC as Receiver of the Columbian Bank and Trust Company v. McCaffree, et al.
Filed August 9, 2011 in the U.S. District Court for the District of Kansas

The complaint brought simple negligence, gross negligence and breach of fiduciary duty claims against officer-directors and outside directors. All directors were on the Directors Loan Committee ("DLC"), the committee that approved the loss loans cited in the complaint. The FDIC sought damages from the defendants in the precise amount of the loss loans, $52 million. The bank failed with $752 million in assets and cost the DIF $60 million.

The board failed to supervise, manage and direct the business affairs of the bank to ensure compliance with the by-laws of the bank or prudent principles of banking.

The FDIC claimed the directors failed to heed warnings of bank supervisory authorities. Regulators warned the defendants that the bank's loan policies were inadequate and that the loan portfolio contained substantial inherent risks as a result of the bank's 80% concentration in commercial and CRE loans. Moreover, the regulators noted that the bank's risk levels had increased because of rapid loan growth in brokered and out-of-territory loans and the bank's loan reviews were insufficient considering the complexity of its lending.

The bank routinely made 100% financing loans to large borrowers. A number of these borrowers ultimately defaulted on their loans, which resulted in defaults that were not secured by collateral. One such borrower was a public company that disclosed its financial problems in a public 10-K; the bank continued to loan to the distressed company after the problems were disclosed. The FDIC alleged reckless and gross misconduct in lending to this borrower.

The FDIC cited the following issues with each loss loan: improper valuation of collateral; insufficient income statement verification; and inadequate monitoring to ensure completion of projects.

The bank extended credit in violation of the bank's written loan policies. The FDIC claimed the bank permitted unsafe and unsound concentrations of credit, provided financing for speculative ventures in which the borrowers invested little or no security, and extended credit to borrowers who were not creditworthy or were known to be in financial difficulty.

The FDIC alleged negligence by the board in allowing credit to be extended without adequately analyzing cash flow, debt service coverage and other critical financial information.

The board negligently relied on a credit memorandum without conducting adequate diligence. The FDIC claimed the memo, produced by a large borrower that had become insolvent, raised significant financing discrepancies with one of the bank's largest loan portfolios.

Generally, the FDIC cited the improper use of interest reserves and interest capitalization as negligent because of the discrepancies in financial statements the misuse created.

The FDIC claimed the directors failed to "review carefully each report of examination of Columbian's affairs as made by the regulatory authorities and to carry out the directions and instructions contained in such reports of examination and to establish and maintain procedures to ensure no recurrence of any deficiencies set forth therein."

FDIC as Receiver of Silverton Bank v. Bryan, et al.
Filed August 22, 2011 in the U.S. District Court for the Northern District of Georgia

The FDIC brought the complaint against officers, inside and outside directors, and an insurance company for negligence, gross negligence, breaches of fiduciary duties, and waste. The bank approved loss loans in the amount of $71 million. The FDIC sued to recover the precise amount of the loss loans. The bank failed with $4.1 billion in assets at a cost of $386 million to the DIF.

"This case presents a text book example of officers and directors of a financial institution being asleep at the wheel and robotically voting for approval of transactions without exercising any business judgment in doing so."

The FDIC claimed the board was on notice of specific issues. When the OCC reviewed the bank's application to convert to a national bank charter, it gave three MRAs to the bank: resolve the CRE concentration to a more acceptable level; revisit its plan to expand and grow to ensure it makes economic sense; and develop a comprehensive capital plan to meet regulatory obligations. The bank failed to obey these directives.

A large portion of managers' compensation was based on growth and expansion. Growth goals were heavily advanced as the bank wanted to become the largest nationally-chartered banker's bank in the country. To push the bank's growth strategy, loan officers were encouraged to generate loans and were rewarded with bonuses. Loan officers received incentive compensation for creating bad loans.

The bank embarked on a course of rapid growth in the real estate construction and investment areas in markets nationwide. The bank's total assets grew from $2 billion as of December 31, 2006 to $3.2 billion as of December 31, 2008. During this time, the bank overly relied on brokered deposits, which grew to $1 billion by December 31, 2008 and then to $1.4 billion by March 31, 2009.

Despite a weakening CRE market and residential real estate market volatility, the bank pursued an aggressive growth plan well past 2007 with the intent to grow out of their problems.

The bank ignored regulatory guidance. The OCC's 2006-46 Bulletin set forth that CRE lending was not to exceed 300% of a bank's capital. The bank's CRE lending ratio to capital was 1,279%.

The bank had significant weaknesses in loan underwriting, credit administration, and a complete disregard of a declining economy. The FDIC claimed the reckless manner in which loans were underwritten caused loans to be highly susceptible to negative changes in the real estate market. The board's conduct was especially egregious because they failed to correct their behavior when the economy began to decline.

Regulators found that: 1) board oversight of the lending area were inadequate; loan staffing levels were inadequate; 2) capital levels were deficient given the bank's high and increasing risk profile; 3) the quality of the loan portfolio was deficient; 4) the board and management did not effectively plan, assess, and manage portfolio concentrations; and, 5) earnings were insufficient to support continued operations and to maintain appropriate capital and ALLL levels."

The board authorized wasteful spending. The bank employed eight private pilots to carry directors and prospective clients to meetings and other locations. The bank spent nearly $62,000 annually on the shareholder meeting. In addition, the bank hosted a luxurious "Executive Management Conference" for its banking customers at the Ritz Carlton at a yearly cost of about $4 million.

FDIC as Receiver of Corn Belt Bank and Trust v. Stark, et al. Filed March 1, 2011 in the U.S. District Court for the Central District of Illinois

FDIC brought the complaint against two inside director-officers and two outside directors who sat on loan committees. The complaint alleged negligence under state law and gross negligence under federal law against all defendants. The inside directors were also sued specifically for the loss loans for failure to administer and oversee adequate lending procedures and to protect security interests. The FDIC sought to recover $10.4 million in losses resulting in the cited loss loans. The bank failed with $260.2 million in assets and cost the DIF an estimated $79.7 million.

The FDIC claimed the board failed to adequately inform themselves of the relevant risks of CRE lending and acted recklessly in approving five high-risk CRE loans as members of the board's loan committee.

The specific loss loans cited in the complaint were improperly underwritten and extended 100 percent financing to out of state, start-up businesses; the loans were primarily secured by rapidly depreciating semi-tractors.

The two inside directors unilaterally approved and funded one loss loan after the loan committee tabled its approval. The two failed to ensure that: the loan was properly administered; the bank monitored and protected its security interests in collateral; and that the loan had adequate maintenance reserves to protect against default.

The ROEs for the bank, from 2003-2008, reflected that the bank failed to address recurring criticisms by examiners regarding imprudent lending practices, including the failure to properly underwrite, manage and administer existing credit relationships.

CRE loan concentrations equaled 307 percent of its Tier 1 Capital, and 60 percent of its loans were adversely classified. The bank reported a loss of $18.1 million primarily from imprudently made commercial loans. The FDIC noted the lending in this area was unsafe and that the board knew it was unsafe yet continued to make the loans.

Specifically, one loss loan had obvious and disclosed issues with borrower capacity. Regulators warned the board that the loan's weaknesses included the fact that they provided 100 percent financing to a start-up business located outside of the Bank's geographical area, and that the loan would be secured by the business assets, rolling stock, deposit accounts, and guarantees that were limited to only 12 percent of the debt.

Board members failed to ensure that borrowers had sufficient maintenance reserves deposited with the bank as required by the loan terms, and by failing to ensure that the bank monitored and controlled the titles to collateral.

The board was warned about the issues in multiple ROEs and MOUs beginning in 2007. The relevant MOUs sought to fix risky loan concentrations and correct violations of banking laws and regulations including capital requirements. The FDIC claimed the bank's noncompliance was gross negligence because they were on notice of the issues.

The FDIC claimed that although the bank had sound loan policies, the directors did not conduct sufficient diligence to ensure the loans they approved were in compliance with the bank's policies.

FDIC as Receiver of Wheatland Bank v. Spangler, et al.
Filed May 5, 2011 in the U.S. District Court for the Northern District of Illinois

The complaint charged gross negligence, negligence, breach of fiduciary duties, and failure to supervise. The defendants are separated into two groups based on whether they were members of the loan committee or not. Three members of the loan committee were outside directors. Four defendants were not members of the loan committee and were outside directors but owned substantial amounts of stock in the bank. The FDIC sought to recover $22 million as a result of the loss loans. The bank failed with assets of $441.6 million and a loss to the Deposit Insurance Fund currently estimated at $136.9 million.

The FDIC cited expansive growth without the requisite experience and oversight necessary to conduct safe and sound lending. The bank had $401 million in loans, almost five times the amount promised in the business plan provided to state and federal regulators. Rapid loan growth compromised credit underwriting and credit administration, which eventually led to loan losses that depleted bank capital.

Generally, the board increased the bank's risk exposure by failing to implement prudent underwriting, risk management and credit administration practices, by failing to follow the bank's written loan policies, and by failing to properly supervise, manage, and oversee the bank's lending operations.

ADC and CRE loans represented over 1000% of bank capital in 2008 (roughly 700% in ADC loans and 300% in CRE loans). This concentration was unacceptable and against federal and state bank regulations. Peer institutions maintained concentration levels at only about 200% of bank capital. Moreover, a small group of borrowers represented 97% of bank capital, above the recommended percentage. FDIC cited these concentrations as unacceptable risk and noted the board was on notice that the concentrations should have been decreased.

Bank examiners repeatedly warned the bank about its excessive and careless growth. In multiple ROEs, the FDIC instructed the bank to decrease its concentration of ADC and CRE loans.

The FDIC suggested the bank increase its underwriting capacity and procedures to ensure complete documentation of income and credit worthiness, proper collateral valuation, improve its capital ratios, and retain qualified management.

The complaint alleged that the board should have increased its participation in the lending process, restrict total asset growth, reduce all loan concentrations, and revise and improve its lending policies. The board failed to adequately implement these suggested changes.

"The Director Defendants failed to properly supervise and oversee the Bank's lending operations. The Loss Loans were poorly underwritten and made in violation of the Bank's loan policies. The Director Defendants permitted loans to be made to favored shareholders and borrowers on terms that were preferential, abusive and harmful to the financial interests of the Bank. And they permitted the Bank to embark on an overly aggressive and risky lending strategy, which produced dangerous concentrations of CRE and ADC loans."

The board failed to supervise the lending process or loan officers. The FDIC claimed this was particularly egregious given its strong and repeated regulatory warnings to the board to get the bank's growth and underwriting procedures under control.

FDIC as Receiver of Cooperative Bank v. Rippy, et al.
Filed August 10, 2011 in the U.S. District Court for the Eastern District of North Carolina

The FDIC brought the complaint against officer-directors and outside directors for breach of fiduciary duties and gross and simple negligence. Most defendants were outside directors who sat on the loan committee responsible for approving the loss loans. The FDIC sought to recover damages of $33 million relating to the loss loans. The complaint separated claims for each loan against individual directors instead of claiming liability against all directors for all the loss loans. The bank failed with $970 million in assets at an estimated cost to the DIF of $217 million.

The bank concentrated lending in high risk ADC and CRE loans. The bank's ADC loan concentration grew from 326% of total capital in December 2005 to 469% of total capital in December 2007. In its peer group, ADC loans comprised 104% of total capital in December 2005 and 124% of total capital in December 2007.

Rather than employing methods to properly monitor and mitigate the risks associated with the highly speculative lending in which the bank was engaging, the board permitted a lax loan approval process which did not include a formal loan committee to meet, review and analyze the loans being made. The process allowed for credit renewals without adequate income verification, collateral inspection, or sufficient loan underwriting analysis.

The bank implemented a system of nine different lending limits that required only specific board member approval for all but one level. Full board approval was only required when loan's went up to the bank's legal lending limit. The FDIC claimed this was gross negligence because it failed to manage obvious risks that regulators warned were unreasonable.

The bank did not establish repayment programs on many delinquent loans and allowed the bank to become overextended, resulting in excessive credit concentrations in high risk loans, excessive loan delinquencies, excessive problem assets, violations of laws and regulations, and insufficient capital to operate the bank sufficiently.

The FDIC claimed the directors were on notice of potential issues because examiners questioned the bank's goal of reaching $1 billion in assets and raised concerns about the bank's liquidity and loan concentrations in real estate construction, development loans and beach resort properties.

The FDIC identified specific underwriting weaknesses: loans were made with little or no hard borrower equity required; analysis of the borrower's or guarantor's contingent liabilities was not performed; and stale financials and credit memoranda were relied upon to approve loans. Previously identified underwriting and administration weaknesses were not being resolved.

The compliant noted that examiners identified significant weaknesses, including liberal renewal and extension practices; inadequate analysis of the borrower's repayment capacity; inadequate borrower equity in real estate projects; over-reliance on collateral as the primary source of repayment; renewing credits without sufficient current financial information; inadequate real estate appraisals and the residential lot loan program.

FDIC as Receiver of Westsound Bank v. Johnson, et al.
Filed November 18, 2011 in the U.S. District Court for the
Western District of Washington

FDIC brought the complaint against insider officer-director (Chairman and CEO) and outside directors who served on the director loan committee for breach of fiduciary duties and gross and simple negligence. The complaint made general claims against all defendants and brought specific claims regarding loss loans and insider loans against a subset of the outside directors and inside directors. The complaint sought to recover $15 million from losses relating to the loss loans. The bank failed with $334.6 million in assets at a cost of $106.4 million to the DIF.

The bank's underwriting process was problematic and lacked proper director supervision. According to the bank's loan policies, all loans over $100,000 were subject to director loan committee approval, but only one quarter of the loss loans were submitted to the director loan committee for approval.

The FDIC cited other issues including incomplete applications, LTV ratios that were dangerously high, failure to undertake appraisals of collateral, and failure to meet required debt coverage ratios. Further, the directors' responsibilities, such as ensuring sound underwriting principles and creating an adequate risk management structure were improperly delegated to low level managers.

The bank had an automated loan approval process for residential loans that could be easily manipulated by loan officers to allow any loan to be approved regardless of the safety of the loan. The FDIC claimed the bank improperly relied on the automated system. The directors were aware of this but did nothing to change the system or enforce greater oversight.

The compensation system awarded high volume production of new loans regardless of the financial soundness of the loans. Coupled with the abuse mentioned above, this created terrible incentives to cheat the system and be rewarded financially for doing so.

The bank overvalued collateral on CRE loans and approved loans with very high LTV ratios. The collateral was usually not properly appraised and was typically inflated to increase lending capacity for each project. CRE loans routinely surpassed the 85% threshold set out in the bank's lending policy. Further, ADC and CRE loan concentration were cited at dangerously high levels.

Regulatory warnings were routinely ignored by the directors and officers. A few issues that were cited were the overemphasis on asset growth, the bank's liquidity problem with capital to loan ratios, improper underwriting policies cited above, and the heavy concentration of risky ADC/CRE loans. The bank also ignored a C&D order.

The FDIC claimed the bank's lending procedures lacked appropriate checks and balances and rewarded irresponsible lending. "The defendants delegated virtually all of their responsibilities over the bank's residential construction lending function to lower level underwriters and loan officers." Specifically, the board relied on an automated system for loan approvals, failed to implement layers of review to approve and properly administer loans, and did not analyze CRE/ADC concentrations.

The bank's financial and capital deficiencies were masked by the excessive use of interest reserves. The FDIC took issue with this practice and claimed it was deceptive and manipulative.

FDIC as Receiver of First National Bank of Nevada v. Dorris, et al.
Filed August 23, 2011 in the U.S. District Court for the District of Arizona

Note: Case has been settled. The complaint was brought against two inside director-officers for gross and simple negligence as well as breach of fiduciary duties of care. The FDIC sought damages to be determined at trial but claimed the FDIC lost an estimated $193 million. The bank failed with $3.4 billion in assets and was purchased by Mutual of Omaha Bank. However, the estimated cost to the DIF was $862 million.

The FDIC claimed the bank concentrated its lending in Alt-A loans that were inherently risky. Despite record returns in the short-term, the strategy was reckless because the loans ended in massive losses when the real estate market softened. The terms of these loans "guaranteed" high default rates in the future and the FDIC made the directors aware of the concerns.

The bank's primary loan portfolios were dependent on perpetually increasing real estate prices, a phenomenon the FDIC claims had never happened before and that prudent directors should have known would not happen. Moreover, many loans showed no ability to be repaid but were funded and approved by the board.

FDIC cited the bank's improper underwriting policies such as not obtaining proper income verifications or allowing managers and analysts to conduct improper collateral appraisals. The bank also failed to implement risk management schemes to mitigate the risks of layered and high-risk loans.

The division charged with issuing Alt-A loans did not follow the bank's own underwriting and quality assurance policies. The division recklessly issued loans to create the growth volume preferred by the board. This was cited as negligent and reckless behavior because almost 85% of the bank's lending was permitted to be concentrated in Alt-A loans.

The FDIC claimed that the board had a non-delegable duty to establish safe and sound lending policies for loan approval and underwriting. Directors delegated the duty of establishing loan approval and lending policies to lower level managers. The bank and the board also allowed investors to set lending policies that were unreasonable and not in accordance with regulatory suggestions.

Regulators consistently warned the bank and the board about its Wholesale Loan Division, the division in charge of overseeing and initiating the Alt-A loss loans. The warnings were ignored and no changes were implemented. The FDIC claimed that any activity subsequent to the warnings constituted gross negligence. The warnings came as early as August 2005. In October 2007, the bank received a CAMELS 4 rating for weakness in oversight and risky lending policies.

FDIC as Receiver for Country Bank v. Hawker, et al.
Filed January 27, 2012 in the U.S. District Court for the Eastern District of California

The complaint alleged breach of fiduciary duties and simple negligence, but no claims of gross negligence or intent. All of the defendants were director-officers, or inside directors. The FDIC sought damages of $42 million resulting from the loss loans cited in the complaint. The bank failed with $1.7 billion in assets at an estimated cost of $135 million to the DIF.

The FDIC claimed the board members approved loans that violated the bank's internal lending policy guidelines. The loans approved contained substandard evaluation of projects, borrowers, and collateral. Loan files "lacked sensitivity analyses, failed to include sound cash flow analyses, failed to evaluate 'what if' scenarios affecting cash flows, failed to compare actual cash flows against *pro forma* projections, and failed to specific secondary repayment sources."

The complaint alleged imprudent growth strategy as a major cause of the bank's failure. The bank had a goal to achieve unreasonable growth and the board encouraged this goal by not implementing and overseeing proper underwriting functions. The board failed to ensure reasonable credit and financial analyses of prospective borrowers and projects.

The bank had issues with documentation requirements for the loss loans. Specific loans were approved despite insufficient guarantors required by the bank's lending policy. The bank approved ADC loans for projects that had insufficient cash flow, collateral, and inadequate financial analysis.

In 2007, the board was on notice that the real estate market was soft and was contracting in the local area. Instead of ensuring loan quality and prudent lending processes, the bank and the board continued to make high-risk loans. Regulators warned the bank that its loan concentrations and underwriting failures were significant risks to the bank's health.

The bank relied on inadequate financial support as to the primary and secondary sources of repayment for many loans at a time when the bank's outstanding credit to borrowers was overextended, under collateralized and highly concentrated in high risk development loans. The complaint cited these issues as negligent and a breach of fiduciary duty. The board failed to investigate the loans before approval. Also, the board failed to take into account the overall health of the bank when approving each loan. The FDIC claimed these were essential duties that should have been completed by the board.

The FDIC alleged the board failed to use "skill and diligence in the performance of their duties, especially in connection with the bank's CRE and development lending functions, including the duty to supervise adequately those employees of the Bank under their supervision and responsibility."

FDIC as Receiver for Bank of Asheville v. Greenwood, et al.
Filed December 29, 2011 in the U.S. District Court for the
Western District of North Carolina

The complaint was brought against one director-officer and six outside directors that either served as chairman of the board at one point or were on committees such as the board's audit committee, executive committee, and bank's loan committee. The complaint cited simple negligence, gross negligence and breach of fiduciary duties against all the defendants. The FDIC sought $6.8 million in damages from the loss loans cited in the complaint. The bank failed with $195 million in assets at a cost of $56 million to the DIF.

The FDIC claimed the defendants, as caretakers of the bank's lending function, failed to implement credit risk management policies and procedures commensurate with the inherent risks associated with a rapidly expanding and heavily concentrated loan portfolio.

The complaint alleged the underwriting process was insufficient because commercial loan borrowers were only required to submit interim financial statements annually, rather than quarterly as was required by the bank's previous underwriting policy. Moreover, the maximum LTV for commercial mortgages was increased from 75% to 80% of the lower of the purchase price or appraised value. Finally, construction loans were excepted from the written take-out requirement.

The loan committee did not have the benefit of reviewing verifying documentation such as borrower/guarantor financial statements, appraisal reviews and project feasibility studies. The practice of approving loans via email also prevented any meaningful discussion between committee members and severely limited members' abilities to conduct a complete and objective overview of the factors necessary to make informed decisions regarding the extension of credit.

The bank focused its lending growth on interest only, high risk, and CRE loans. This growth strategy was seen as particularly risky and the FDIC claimed the board was negligent in allowing the bank to embark on this policy.

To establish gross negligence, the FDIC claimed the board was put on notice and intentionally disregarded regulators' warnings over a span of approximately three years. Regulators (and auditors) identified an increasing loan concentration in CRE lending, and noted deficiencies in the monitoring and reporting of this concentration, as noted above. Together, CRE and business loans represented over 90% of all loans; CRE loans represented 470% of total risk-based capital.

The defendants failed to properly supervise the bank's mostly inexperienced and under-qualified loan officers or to ensure sound underwriting practices were enforced. Specific underwriting weaknesses included: inaccurate and inadequately supported loan presentations, inadequate analyses of borrower and guarantor contingent liabilities, inadequate verification of collateral value or feasibility of speculative projects, and no clear purpose for use of loan proceeds.

The bank used interest reserves to mask growing loan quality issues and liberal renewal policy further contributed to the masking of declines in loan quality. The policy required interest only loans to be approved and put on repayment plans after the initial time period, but the bank's loan committee routinely reauthorized interest only loans via email without credit analysis.

FDIC as Receiver for R-G Premier Bank of Puerto Rico v. Galan-Alvarez, et al.
Filed January 18, 2012 in the U.S. District Court for the District of Puerto Rico

The FDIC brought the complaint against nineteen former directors (inside and outside) and officers, seventeen of their spouses, and seventeen related conjugal partnerships, and their director and officer liability insurer. The claims were based on gross negligence and breach of fiduciary duties. There were no simple negligence claims. The FDIC sought damages of at least $257 million. The bank failed with $5.92 billion in assets at a cost to the DIF of $1.46 billion.

The FDIC claimed the board was grossly negligent because it failed to exercise due care nor any business judgment in approving obviously risky and deficiently underwritten loans. Moreover, the board negligently failed to inform themselves about, and to exercise adequate oversight over, the bank's lending function. Essentially, too much authority was delegated to loan officers.

"By ignoring the obvious risks of injury to the Bank from specific loans which they knew or should have known were extremely unlikely to be paid back, and also the equally clear risks of injury to the Bank from the Bank's inappropriate lending structure, the Directors and Officers breached their fiduciary duties of care to the Bank."

The board established a management structure that gave one director-officer complete control over the bank's credit and risk management departments. Credit risk personnel ultimately answered to the chief loan producer, and could not effectively voice concerns about underwriting loans or borrowers' creditworthiness. Regulators repeatedly warned the board that its refusal to segregate loan production from credit risk management posed significant risk to the bank.

"Board failed to institute effective loan reviews, critically undermining its own ability to monitor the health and quality of its rapidly expanding commercial loan portfolio. Management approved many policy exceptions on a loan-by-loan basis with no mechanism to track the aggregate level or materiality." The bank's own policy prohibited more than three extensions for one loan. However, extensions were granted whenever an officer completed an extension form. The FDIC cited this practice as reckless and careless, two elements used to support gross negligence.

Regulators repeatedly warned the bank of its underwriting and credit policy deficiencies. The bank was warned that its loan concentrations and LTV ratios were dangerously high. The bank suffered decreased CAMELS ratings and had multiple C&D orders filed against them as early as 2006. However, the board did not adequately respond to regulators' complaints.

The FDIC alleged that the bank ignored its own policies for approvals and the board did not implement sufficient controls to oversee the lending function. The board did not put a proper policy in place to ensure sufficient underwriting and loan committees were reckless in their approval of the loss loans.

The directors were accused of individually approving the loss loans over the course of two years. The complaint did not separate individual loans against specific directors, however.

FDIC as Receiver of Westernbank Puerto Rico v. Garcia, et al.
Filed January 20, 2012 in the U.S. District Court for the
District of Puerto Rico

The complaint brought claims of gross negligence, breach of fiduciary duty, and adverse domination. No simple negligence was claimed. The complaint listed director officers, and both inside and outside directors. Also, the complaint lists the spouses and conjugal partnerships of the defendants as required by Puerto Rico law. The FDIC sought to recover approximately $176 million resulting from the loss loans cited in the complaint. The bank failed with $11.9 billion in assets at an estimated cost of $3.31 billion to the DIF.

FDIC cited the following violations in its case summary: (1) violations of the bank's LTV ratio limits; (2) lack of required borrower equity; (3) inadequate real estate appraisals; (4) insufficient analyses of collateral or inadequate collateral; (5) insufficient borrower repayment information and repayment sources; and (6) the questionable character of the borrower or guarantor.

Additionally, the defendants repeatedly increased, extended, and/or renewed expired and deteriorating loans to enable continued funding of interest reserves.

A former director failed to disclose his substantial personal financial interest in a $12 million CRE loan before its approval, in violation of bank policies and federal regulations.

Specifically, the FDIC noted that the bank's CRE and construction loans lacked financial support, cash flow and debt service analyses, exceeded LTV ratio limits, and were based on faulty appraisals. Construction loans were extended, administered, and funded in violation of key loan approval terms and bank policies such as inadequate appraisals and income documentation.

The FDIC alleged certain directors were aware as early as 2005 that the bank had issues with underwriting and administering loans. One director advised the board and officers to cease lending until the administrative errors could be corrected. Yet the same director approved further loss loans. The FDIC used these facts to establish gross negligence.

The board approved, increased, renewed and/or extended the loss loans in the face of mounting examiner and auditor warnings regarding the commercial loan portfolio. In 2005, the ROE cited management's failure to correct deficiencies in loan administration and review cited in the prior year's examination. In 2006, the bank's auditors warned management of "significant deficiencies," including insufficient analysis and documentation of impaired loans.

In 2008, examiners adversely classified $1.8 billion of the bank's assets, a more than 300 percent increase from the prior year. The examiners also criticized the bank's continued funding of interest reserves on troubled projects. Despite these warnings, the board approved, increased and renewed loans in violation of the bank's approval policies, federal safety and soundness regulations, and prudent banking practices. A Form S-K in 2007 acknowledged the bank's underwriting shortcomings.

The FDIC alleged the directors were responsible for not heeding examiner and auditor warnings and correcting those deficiencies.

FDIC as Receiver for Silver State Bank v. Johnson, et al. Filed February 9, 2012 in the U.S. District Court for the District of Nevada

The FDIC brought the complaint against one director-officer and three officers for gross negligence and breaches of fiduciary duties; no simple negligence is alleged. Two of the officers were fired by the board prior to the complaint being filed. The FDIC sought to recover $86 million related to the loss loans cited in the complaint. The bank failed with close to $2.0 billion in assets at an estimated cost to the DIF of $450 to $550 million.

The FDIC cited the aggressive funding of high risk ADC loans with brokered deposits as particularly reckless.

The bank grew its ADC loans each year from 2006-2008, despite clear indications that the market was collapsing. Other similarly sized banks had ceased ADC loans in the region completely. The first indications of a declining real estate market and explicit warnings to the bank were made in mid-2005. One officer has admitted to knowing the local real estate market was a "house of cards."

The FDIC asserted that the bank's compensation structure exacerbated the situation because it rewarded quantity over quality loans. Risk and creditworthiness were disregarded for compensation purposes. Loan officers received a 10% bonus of all fee income earned from newly originated loans.

The growth and sources of income for the bank were extremely high compared to the bank's peers. For example, the bank ranked in the upper 95th percentile for fee and interest income, as well as asset growth rate.

In 2007, regulators told the bank that it had no formal policy regarding loan disbursements, there were too many employees with the ability to sign cashier's checks, and many construction loans were funded without using a standard voucher company that would have included site inspections.

The complaint claimed ADC loan concentration was dangerously high and remained so during 2006-2007 when the real estate market was substantially retracting. Additionally, many of the loan officers had no experience in credit analysis; they were simply charged with making new loans.

Regulators warned the bank and the board of the high concentration in ADC and speculative loans. The bank continued to increase the volume of ADC lending to reach its $2 billion in assets goal. Regulators also questioned the collateral pledged to a large number of construction and development loans. The valuation of the collateral was not adequate. Regulators also suggested the bank not use interest reserves and to adopt written policies regarding proper usage of interest reserves. ADC and CRE loans were 898% of total risk based capital, an amount strongly discouraged by regulators.

The bank's loan policies and procedures were sufficient to safely underwrite a loan and ensure credit worthiness. However, despite the bank's strong internal controls, the policies were neither followed nor enforced by managers. Loan officers and credit analysts routinely disregarded internal controls regarding income statements and creditworthiness.

FDIC as Receiver for Community Bank & Trust v. Miller, et al.
Filed February 24, 2012 in the U.S. District Court for the Northern District of Florida

The complaint was filed against two officers, only one was a director-officer. The FDIC alleged simple and gross negligence, as well as breach of fiduciary duty against both parties. Interestingly, the filing occurred in Georgia after the *Integrity Bank* order dismissed the FDIC's simple negligence claims. The FDIC sought to recover $11 million from the loss loans cited in the complaint. The bank failed with $1.2 billion in assets at a cost of $354 million to the DIF.

The FDIC claimed the defendants breached their fiduciary duties by approving loans that violated the bank's loan policy. Loans were approved without verified borrower financial information, adequate appraisals, and/or authorization to exceed his individual lending authority.

The inside director was negligent in failing to supervise the officers and implement corrective measures after notice in January 2006 that the officer defendant was violating the bank's loan policy and approving loans with underwriting deficiencies.

The loans at issue here were loans that were originated by the officer defendant named in the complaint. The loans were made to one customer under specific circumstances. The customer would facilitate loans for his clients in a program called the Home Funding Loan Program (HFLP) loans. "HFLP loans were high-risk, short-term bridge loans that were intended to be repaid when the investor/purchaser obtained permanent financing. The majority of these HFLP loans funded purchases of investment single family residences in the Atlanta low-end housing market, including funds for alleged repairs, renovations, and improvements."

The officer defendant approved HFLP loans without obtaining signed or completed financial statements, without appraisals, and in excess of the bank's LTV ratio limit. He also approved HFLP loans where the collateral was outside the bank's lending territory and authorized out-of-territory loans as both the primary loan officer and senior lending officer. The FDIC claimed it was negligent oversight and an unsafe lending practice to allow one officer to approve loans unilaterally without review by the board.

Although regulators were never involved in warning the bank of its underwriting violations and risky lending, the bank was made aware of the HFLP situation. One supervisor specifically wrote two memos on the subject to upper level management and the loan review committee. Despite these warnings, the bank increased lending in this area almost 400% over about one year. When a formal review was conducted, the board outlined the issues and suggested making changes to the loan policy, but ultimately decided not to do so because the officer promised to correct the situation.

The bank had a sound loan policy with effective controls. The FDIC did not take issue with the bank's policy nor the board as a whole.

FDIC as Receiver for Florida Community Bank v. Price, et al. Filed March 13, 2012 in the U.S. District Court for the Middle District of Florida

The complaint alleged negligence under state law against both an inside director-officer and a number of outside directors who sat on the board loan committee. Further, members on the bank's audit committee were also sued because the audit committee reviewed actions by the loan committee. The agency also claimed gross negligence under federal law against all directors. The FDIC sought damages in excess of $62 million resulting from the loss loans cited in the complaint. The bank failed with approximately $870 million in total assets at a cost of $349.1 million to the DIF.

The FDIC claimed the directors ignored regulators' warnings about risky loan strategies and the practice of approving ADC and CRE loans without proper underwriting procedures such as verifying income or valuation of collateral.

The bank was operating on dangerously low capital to asset ratios and maintained little to no liquidity because of the lending strategy that focused on ADC and CRE loans. The FDIC called this strategy negligent and claimed that a reasonably prudent board member exercising sufficient diligence would not have approved the strategy or the loans.

The FDIC noted that the board failed to question management's strategies, even in spite of regulators' warnings. Moreover, the FDIC claimed the board should not have allowed Price, an executive officer and board member, to unilaterally approve loans without the board's consent or knowledge. By allowing him to do so, the board was grossly negligent. The agency claimed that the board should not have allowed any loans to be approved by Price without the board's review or approval.

LTV ratios on the loss loans were outside the bank's lending policy limitations. Despite knowing this, the board chose to approve the loss loans. The FDIC claimed the board was responsible for investigating whether these loans were compliant with the bank's policies. The failure to do so was negligent, according to the complaint.

The FDIC noted that the bank made ADC and CRE loans to consumers in markets with which the bank was unfamiliar. These out of market loans were seen as negligent and unsafe because the board was warned about the risks associated with the markets and the particular loans.

The board did not review the loan policy annually as required by the bank's policies. The board made periodic amendments but never did a thorough review of the bank's loan policy. The FDIC saw this as negligent oversight. Additionally, the board gave extensive powers to loan officers that resulted in less oversight and insufficient review of proposed loans.

The FDIC claimed the bank disregarded its commitments to the agency to make necessary changes. Despite entering a Stipulation and Consent Agreement to halt ADC and CRE lending, the bank continuously pursued a policy of risky lending and the board even adopted a formal amendment to its loan policy to originate ADC and out of market loans.

FDIC as Receiver for Freedom Bank of Georgia v. Adams, et al.
Filed March 2, 2012 in the U.S. District Court for the Northern District of Georgia

The complaint was brought against directors who were members of the board loan committee for violations of state law negligence, breach of fiduciary duties, and gross negligence under federal law. One director was an inside, officer-director, while another defendant was simply a loan officer. However, three directors were named as defendants who were not members of the loan committee. The FDIC sought damages of $11 million from the loss loans cited in the complaint. The bank failed with $173 million in assets at a cost of $36.2 million to the DIF.

FDIC claimed that CRE loans were inherently risky and that fluctuations in this market were cyclical and therefore foreseeable by reasonably prudent bankers. Further, the agency claimed that ADC loans were even more risky than CRE loans.

The complaint alleged the board did not implement sound risk management, loan underwriting, or credit administration practices to accommodate for the types of loans the bank originated. The board consistently chose to delegate its loan approval duties to officers and a small group of directors by increasing the loan amounts that needed loan committee approval.

CRE loans were over 700% and ADC loans were over 400% of the bank's capital. These levels were dangerously high and regulators made the board and officers aware of these concerns in 2008.

The FDIC took issue with the bank's loan policy because it did not establish specific limits on loan concentrations, nor did it limit ADC or CRE loans in any meaningful way. The policy also did not require a global cash flow inquiry.

The above loan concentrations alone were an issue. Yet, when combined with the fact that the board did not implement any matter of protective measures, the board was grossly negligent and violated its fiduciary duties of oversight and care. The board did not establish proper loss reserves for these risky loans after accounts became delinquent.

The board approved loans with outdated financial statements and inadequate income to support repayment of the terms of the loans. The FDIC claimed the bank's own internal records regarding the loss loans made it clear that certain loans were high risk and that borrowers and their pledged capital were not sufficient to support repayment or servicing of the loans.

The FDIC claimed that in many of the loss loans, internal financial analysis determined the loans were not financially stable and were inherently risky. However, the board approved the loans to support its aggressive growth strategy.

FDIC as Receiver for Broadway Bank v. Giannoulias, et al.
Filed March 7, 2012 in the U.S. District Court for the Northern District of Illinois

The complaint was brought against seven directors; one was an officer-director, and two were officers who did not sit on the board but were members of the loan committee. All directors and officers approved the loss loans in question. The complaint alleged gross and simple negligence, as well as breaches of fiduciary duties. The FDIC sought damages of $20 million resulting from the loss loans cited in the complaint. The bank failed with $1.06 billion in assets at a cost of $391.4 million to the DIF.

The FDIC claimed the directors recklessly implemented a strategy of rapidly growing the bank's assets by approving high-risk loans without regard for appropriate underwriting and credit administration practices, the bank's written loan policies, federal lending regulations and warnings from the bank's regulators.

Starting in January 2007 and continuing through April 2009, the FDIC and other regulators made continuous efforts to curtail the risky lending the bank had pursued in the areas of ADC and CRE loans. Examiners noted weaknesses in loan administration and underwriting, including failing to obtain borrowers' current financial statements and the failure to obtain global cash flow analyses from borrowers with multiple loans.

Examiners criticized the bank's ALLL methodology for "failing to include an impairment analysis and failing to downgrade loans that were classified at previous examinations." Failure to ensure accurate ALLL calculations overstated the bank's financial performance.

The FDIC praised the bank's internal loan policy but noted that the board and officers failed to implement or adhere to the policy in approving the loss loans. "The Loan Policy required diligent underwriting in conformity with state and federal law, close monitoring of concentrations of credit and rigorous documentation and prudent evaluation of borrower and project risk. In approving the Loss Loans, however, Defendants routinely ignored and repeatedly failed to enforce the Loan Policy's provisions. The Bank's loan approval policies also were frequently bypassed."

The bank entered at least one MOU with the FDIC to correct underwriting problems and loan concentrations in risky areas such as ADC and CRE lending. "The regulators provided a sustained and constructive critique of the Bank's operations and, through the MOU, sought a written commitment from Defendants to address the criticisms and reduce the Bank's excessive risk-taking." The FDIC claimed it was gross negligence for the board to not adhere to the MOUs.

The FDIC claimed loan concentrations were allowed to grow essentially without control, a strategy that was noted as unsafe and reckless. The bank's ADC loans were almost 800% of capital while its CRE loans were over 1100% of capital. This was more than triple the concentration of the bank's peer group in the same areas.

The complaint alleged that the bank was lending in new areas without adequate knowledge or risk management policies and expertise. "The risks associated with Broadway's portfolio were exacerbated because many of these projects were located outside of Illinois. The Bank did not have sufficient staff to monitor these out-of-state projects adequately and deferred excessively to its borrowers regarding market evaluations and risk."

FDIC as Receiver for Omni National Bank v. Klein, et al. Filed March 16, 2012 in the U.S. District Court for the Northern District of Georgia

The complaint was brought against three inside director-officers and multiple other officers who were not directors. No outside directors were named in the complaint. The complaint alleged negligence and gross negligence as well as corporate waste. The FDIC sought nearly $37.1 million in damages from the loss loans and wasteful expenditures. The bank failed with $986 million in total assets at a cost of $330.6 million to the DIF.

The FDIC claimed the defendants approved loans despite knowing the risks associated with the loans and violating banking regulations and the bank's internal loan policy. "These violations included, but were not limited to: (1) violations of Loan to One Borrower ("LTOB") limits through use of straw borrowers; (2) violations of Loan to Value ("LTV") ratio limits; (3) failure to obtain appraisals prior to funding and/or acceptance of stale appraisals, re-dated appraisals increased to the needed loan amount, or "drive by" appraisals; (4) lack of required borrower equity or down payment; (5) insufficient borrower credit scores or repayment ability; (6) loans to finance land flips generating seller profits of over ten percent; and (7) multiple loans on foreclosed properties to avoid or delay loss recognition."
The FDIC cited the bank's bonus policy as negligent because it awarded loan origination instead of loan soundness and quality. Year-end bonuses were tied to the number of loans originated and the amount of potential fees and interest the bank could capture off the originated loans.

The bank embarked on a policy to increase real estate secured loans despite knowing in 2006-07 that the residential and commercial real estate market in the bank's lending area was declining. The bank increased risky lending by 300% over the years following 2007. "After the community development lending division (CDLD) stopped lending in December 2007, Omni increased foreclosures and rapidly accumulated OREO properties.

To avoid recognizing significant losses, Omni booked many of the other real estate owned (OREO) properties at inflated "as repaired" values rather than "as is" values, in violation of federal regulations and Bank policies. Additionally, instead of selling the OREO, Klein decided to renovate many of the OREO properties for lease to low income tenants."

The board was made aware of widespread negligent and grossly negligent lending practices in the CDLD, including the following: "use of straw borrowers to circumvent LTOB limits; loans in excess of LTV ratio limits; failure to obtain required appraisals, down payments, or creditworthy borrowers; excessive "land flip" profits by which sellers bought and sold the same property at inflated values, receiving over ten percent profit in violation of Bank policy; and multiple loans to finance sales of properties in increasing amounts to avoid OREO booking and loss recognition."

In 2008, the OCC issued directives to the bank to write down a third of the OREO properties and decreased the bank's composite CAMELS ratings to a 5. Instead of liquidating the additional OREO properties "as-is" to conserve its remaining capital, the bank expended over $12.6 million (38% of the bank's Tier 1 capital) to maintain, rehabilitate, renovate and improve additional OREO properties.

The FDIC did not take issue with the bank's lending policy, however, it noted that the officers did not comply or adhere to the standards outlined in the policy. This was cited as gross negligence.

FDIC as Receiver for Cape Fear Bank v. Coburn, et al.
Filed April 4, 2012 in the U.S. District Court for the Eastern District of North Carolina

The complaint was brought against inside director-officers and outside bank directors for breaches of fiduciary duties, negligence and gross negligence. The FDIC sought to recover $11.2 million as a result of the loss loans cited in the complaint. The bank failed with $492 million in assets at a cost of $141 million to the DIF.

The FDIC claimed the defendants' failure to establish and adhere to sound loan policies and procedures resulted in the approval of poorly underwritten and structured real estate dependent loans, including the loss loans. The agency also noted that the bank decided to continue opening new branch offices despite repeated warnings to stop expansion.

The loss loans, at the time of approval: (a) increased previously criticized concentrations, (b) violated Loan Policy and applicable laws and regulations, (c) lacked proper financial analysis or verification of the creditworthiness of the borrower and/or guarantor, and/or (d) often lacked a proper appraisal of the collateral. The inherent risks created by these improvidently granted loans were magnified when the inevitable slowdown in the real estate market began.

Rather than restricting high risk lending, working out the existing troubled loans, and preserving the bank's capital, the defendants took actions that masked the bank's problems by approving additional loss loans and renewing and making additional loan advances on non-performing loss loans. These were cited as negligent and unsafe banking practices.

The board failed to exercise independent judgment and to act in the best interest of the bank when entering, approving, and ratifying loans. The FDIC noted the board also failed to maintain or require and supervise the maintenance of adequate loan documentation. The board did not exercise due diligence and care in the supervision of the bank's officers and employees. Further, the defendants violated or permitted violation of prudent banking practices by making or permitting loans in which the sale or liquidation of collateral security was the only method by which the loan could be repaid.

The board allowed loans to be made based on grossly inadequate or inaccurate information regarding the finances of the borrower, the value of the collateral, and/or the sources of repayment. The loans were made on an under-secured basis, contrary to prudent banking practice. The FDIC noted the defendants failed to appropriately investigate borrowers' creditworthiness, representations of values contained in the borrowers' financial statements, and the actual value of collateral given as security.

The FDIC noted that the defendants approved loans in excess of 100% financing for speculative ventures and loans with excessive LTV ratios and/or deficient or incomplete appraisals.

The board failed to inform themselves and each other of the true condition of the assets and liabilities of the bank and the nature of its loan portfolio, or to review and inquire adequately into the bank's loan transactions. Further, the FDIC claimed that the board failed to establish or adhere to adequate policies and procedures prescribing the conditions and limitations under which loans could be made and the underwriting and record-keeping which should be undertaken on loans.

The FDIC claimed the defendants were grossly negligent because they failed to establish or adhere to policies responsive to the numerous warnings and criticisms by federal and state banking regulators.

FDIC as Receiver for First Bank of Beverly Hills v. Faigin, et al.
Filed April 20, 2012 in the U.S. District Court for the Central District of California

This complaint was filed against both inside and outside directors of the bank for simple and gross negligence, and breach of fiduciary duties. The inside directors were accused of simple and gross negligence. The outside directors were charged with gross negligence. All defendants were charged with breach of fiduciary duties. The FDIC sought to recover $100.6 million in damages resulting from the loss loans. Eight of the nine loss loans were participation loans with other institutions. The bank failed with $1.5 billion in assets at a cost of $394 million to the DIF.

The FDIC cited the bank's strategy and approval in making high concentrations of CRE and ADC loans allegedly without properly underwriting the loan participations. Credit analysis and valuation of collateral were two areas the FDIC specifically cited as troublesome regarding approval of the loans.
Directors did not properly inform themselves of the risks associated with making the loss loans before the directors approved the loans. The FDIC claimed the directors had an additional duty to investigate the loans before relying on the loan officers' presentation to approve the loans.

The FDIC claimed the directors had a duty to ensure loans were underwritten properly and that loans were approved in accordance with applicable regulations. The FDIC asserted that the loan approvals were continued despite warnings from regulators that the concentrations were unsafe and the approval procedures were reckless.

The FDIC noted that the board did not follow the bank's own lending policies. Loans allegedly were approved despite having insufficient income necessary to repay the loans; many loans had excessive LTV ratios that were inconsistent with the bank's lending policy.

The FDIC specifically cited that the directors relied on loan officers' due diligence and representations instead of conducting diligence themselves. California law protects directors when they reasonably rely on representations by officers regarding business decisions. The complaint stated reliance on internal credit memos was not appropriate because the memos were "facially deficient."

The FDIC cited the improper usage of interest reserves to hide losses. Interest reserves purportedly were used improperly to cover losses on loans or make loans appear to be current by shifting the reserves to show the loans were current.

The complaint alleged that the board ignored federal regulators and were therefore on notice and acting recklessly. Despite regulators' warnings, the FDIC asserts that the board did not reasonably investigate the deficiencies identified in the ROEs.

Defendants allegedly did not conduct proper reviews of the bank's loan policies to ensure the bank's loan policies were being implemented. The FDIC claimed this was negligent oversight because the board did not supervise or ensure safe and sound lending practices were being used by loan officers.

The FDIC claimed that insufficient actions were taken by the board to prevent the reoccurrence of unsafe or unsound banking practices.

FDIC as Receiver for Innovative Bank v. Hong, et al.
Filed May 23, 2012 in the U.S. District Court for the Northern District of California

The complaint was brought against inside director-officers and outside directors.. All defendants were sued for breach of fiduciary duties and gross negligence. The complaint separated the gross negligence claims to bring specific claims against directors. Further, the FDIC brought ordinary negligence claims against the officers only. Finally, one officer was charged with fraud. The FDIC sought to recover $7.1 million from the loss loans cited in the complaint. The bank failed with $268 million in assets at a cost of $37.8 million to the DIF.

The FDIC claimed the director defendants breached their fiduciary duties by failing to supervise the bank's SBA loan program, including not heeding regulators' and internal warnings. Moreover, the directors failed to adopt and implement appropriate SBA policies in response to regulatory criticisms and guidance that the FDIC claimed would have prevented related losses.

The complaint alleged that all defendants were grossly negligent because they failed to: 1) inform themselves about the risks of specific loss loans; 2) ensure loans were properly underwritten or properly secured with collateral; and 3) respond to regulatory and serious internal warnings regarding the risks associated with specific loans and the flawed loan approval and underwriting policies.

The director defendants were specifically charged with separate counts of gross negligence because they did not properly supervise the officers of the bank. The FDIC claimed it was the directors' duty to use ordinary diligence to assess the condition of the bank's business, and to exercise reasonable control over its officers.

Specifically, the FDIC claimed the directors failed to reasonably inform themselves about the lending activities of the officers, and failed to exercise reasonable judgment when approving loans. The failure to oversee the officers was cited as "scant care and a departure from the ordinary standard of care." The FDIC claimed the directors were grossly negligent in overseeing the officers.

The FDIC claimed the directors repeatedly ignored obvious loan policy violations causing loans to be approved that were unsoundly underwritten. This was characterized as gross negligence.

FDIC as Receiver for Community Bank of Arizona v. Jamison, et al.
Filed July 13, 2012 in the U.S. District Court for the District of Arizona

The complaint was brought against inside director officers and four outside directors. The three count charge alleges negligence by the director officers and gross negligence by all defendants. Further, a general breach of fiduciary duties charge is alleged against all defendants. The FDIC sought to recover $11 million is damages resulting from the loss loans cited in the complaint. The bank had $158.5 million in total assets and failed at an estimated cost of $25.5 million to the DIF.

The FDIC claimed that the board simply rubber stamped loan approvals without exercising any oversight or conducting independent diligence. Generally, the loss loans were claimed to have been in violation of the bank's lending policy and sound banking practices. Loans were approved with underwriting discrepancies and against applicable banking regulations.

Specifically, the FDIC claimed the directors: caused the bank to purchase loan interests that did not meet the bank's underwriting policies; failed to conduct financial analyses and appropriate collateral appraisals for specific loan purchases; did not complete borrower and guarantor financial analysis; and failed to accurately calculate or evaluate the bank's high concentration in CRE loans.

The FDIC noted that the bank's lending policy was specific and complete enough to support the board's lending approval function. However, the board did not follow specific written policies such as having loan officers conduct site inspections, completing a financial analysis of commercial real estate loans before approving the loans, and having loans be supported by independent underwriters.

The bank's high number of CRE loans were cited as an issue the board failed to address and compounded by ignoring warnings and concentration limitations. The board originated CRE loans without following proper underwriting procedures and allowed the concentration of CRE loans to exceed 60% of bank lending.

The FDIC claimed the bank ignored regulatory warnings such as published guidance and specific ROEs issued for the bank. Specifically, the bank was warned about its lower level of Tier 1 capital and the risks associated with the high concentration level of CRE loans. Despite the warnings, the bank purchased more troubled loans from other banks in 2008.

Prior to the bank's failure, the FDIC claimed it warned the bank that it had issues with its underwriting documentation. The FDIC claimed there was little oversight by the board and that no independent loan review was undertaken. The FDIC used this to say the board did not reasonably rely on staff because the board was grossly negligent in approving loans with glaring and obvious issues.

FDIC as Receiver for First Piedmont Bank v. Whitley, et al.
Filed July 13, 2012 in the U.S. District Court for the Northern District of Georgia

The complaint was brought against inside and outside directors for gross and simple negligence. Each defendant is charged under state law for ordinary negligence and under federal law for gross negligence. The FDIC sought to recover an amount to be proven at trial resulting from losses caused by improper lending to specific projects. The complaint differs from others in that it does not attach damages to the loss loans explicitly. The bank failed with $201.7 million in total assets at an estimated cost of $71.6 million to the DIF.

The FDIC claimed the directors were grossly negligent in approving ADC loans due to the failure to independently analyze the loans, properly evaluate collateral, and overlooking glaring deficiencies in the presentation of loan materials.

Despite having a strong existing loan policy, the board caused the bank to fail to follow its own LTV ratio on many of the loans it funded and violated its lending policy regarding the loan limits for a single customer. The FDIC claimed this was gross negligence.

The complaint alleged that the board did not ensure the managers or officers complied with existing underwriting policies and bank regulations for individual loans. Also, the bank did not adhere to Tier 1 capital limits.

The FDIC claimed the directors had the duty to ensure that the bank's policies were strictly followed and to take reasonably prudent steps to analyze business decisions so that the bank did not enter into unreasonable transactions. Moreover, the directors had a duty to make sure the bank did not grow at an unsafe pace in areas of lending that were unreasonably risky, and to exercise independent diligence in approving transactions and loans.

The agency alleged that ADC loans were speculative and inherently unsafe. The board should have limited its exposure to this area of lending, especially after regulators warned the bank about its underwriting issues and concentration levels. The FDIC claimed that there is a high correlation between bank failures and high concentrations in ADC loans.

Despite a strong internal policy regarding loan limitations, the board violated the policy and made changes to lending limits that were adverse to ADC loans as a ratio to Tier 1 capital. The FDIC claimed the board should not have adopted this change in policy because doing so was gross negligence.

The board did not ensure that large loans over $250,000 had the proper underwriting components such as an independent credit and collateral evaluation, a practice that was in violation of FDIC regulations.

FDIC as Receiver of IndyMac Bank v. Perry, et al.
Filed July 6, 2011 in the U.S. District Court for the Central District of California

The complaint was brought solely against Michael Perry, CEO and Chairman of the Board for simple negligence and breach of fiduciary duties. The FDIC claimed the loss loans accounted for over $600 million in total losses. The bank had $32 billion in assets when it failed. The FDIC estimated that losses to the DIF were between $4 and $8 billion.

Defendant allowed loan officers to issue billions of dollars in piggyback loans to borrowers for residential property. The FDIC explained the procedure as a first mortgage of up to 80% of the value of the home or collateral and a second mortgage for the remaining 20% of value. The structure left no equity in the specific homes and, thus, insufficient collateral.

Defendant acted negligently as the CEO because he allowed the bank's loans to be made with layers of substantial risk and supported a business model that encouraged risk taking. The bank did not underwrite loans purchased from other generators and had to rely upon what the other generator did or did not do as to underwriting.

76% of all the bank's loans were not properly documented and failed to undertake any proof of borrowers' income. Many of the loans had risky repayment schemes (optional adjustable rates, subprime mortgages) that, in a time of economic decline, increased the likelihood of borrower default.

Many loans were in second position (behind first mortgages) as closed-end, stand-alone second loans or stand-alone HELOCs. In 2007, the real estate market had declining values and there was a substantial risk that loans in second position would become under-secured.

The bank made a high number of loans that were generated or purchased in order to be sold into the secondary market but were held for sale for 90-180 days. The FDIC claimed that during the real estate decline, this holding period became a fundamental problem that created unnecessary risk for the bank because the secondary market was volatile. The bank needed to sell the loans quicker.

The FDIC claimed the bank wrongly emphasized production and market share over credit quality and quality underwriting. Defendant negligently elevated his desire to increase the bank's market share over prudent risk management.

Despite warnings and knowledge of serious problems in both the housing and secondary markets, defendant negligently allowed the bank to generate risky loans during 2006 and 2007 that were intended to be sold into the secondary market. However, the market became volatile and demand for the loan products decreased causing the loans to be reclassified as investment loans and ultimately written off.

The complaint cited emails that showed defendant knew the market was declining but chose to increase lending to gain market share.

FDIC as Receiver of Washington Mutual Bank v. Killinger, et al.
Filed March 16, 2011 in the U.S. District Court for the Western District of Washington

Note: Case has been settled. The complaint was brought against three inside director-officers and two of their spouses (not directors) for simple and gross negligence, breach of fiduciary duties, and fraudulent conveyance. The FDIC sought damages to be decided at trial. The bank failed with $307 billion in assets but was sold to JP Morgan and avoided any costs to the DIF.

Defendants were experienced bankers who knew that WaMu was taking extreme risks when it focused on growing its Held for Investment (HFI) residential mortgage portfolio with multi-risk layered Option ARMs, HELOCs and subprime mortgages. Defendants also knew that strong risk analysis and management was critical to managing this type of higher risk loan portfolio. Option ARMs totaled more than $51 billion and accounted for 50% of the bank's portfolio.

The bank wanted to grow by at least 13% per year and wanted to focus on markets in Florida and California. These markets were hit the hardest by the real estate decline. The directors' attitudes were that above average creation of shareholder value requires significant risk taking. The bank was warned by managers that the growth strategy could cause capital and credit function problems.

The bank concentrated too much lending into Alt-A, subprime and ARMs. The concentrations were much higher than peer institutions and the incentives to create these loans caused the problem to worsen. Many times the bank issued loans with little or no collateral to secure the loans, with the exception of the property itself. HELOCs were also a major portfolio item and over 18% of the bank's HELOCs experienced delinquency. Subprime delinquency was over 25%.

The FDIC noted the defendants were repeatedly warned that robust risk management of Single Family Residential (SFR) lending was especially critical in light of WaMu's sales-driven culture and the Higher Risk Lending Strategy, and that risk managers would need senior management's support to be effective. As experienced bankers, defendants knew or should have known this even if they had not been warned.

The FDIC claimed the board marginalized risk in the face of multiple internal warnings from managers and outside risk consultants. Defendants knowingly suppressed discussions of SFR lending risk in meetings of the Executive Committee. They treated the Chief Enterprise Risk Officer dismissively, excluding him from important meetings, and ultimately terminated him in May 2008. Other senior risk managers also clashed with the board over their attempts to better manage the risks in WaMu's SFR lending.

The bank exhibited major infrastructure problems with technology and integration. This made it difficult for the bank to monitor results and manage lending risks in its HFI portfolio. The bank had separate platforms for its SFR lending, with largely manual rather than computerized processes and had multiple loan origination platforms that were not coordinated.

Regulatory guidance was not followed. Guidance, issued jointly by the FDIC and other federal agencies, addressed option ARMs and other nontraditional loans that allowed borrowers to defer payment of principal and interest. Regulators urged the bank to use risk management practices that the bank ultimately failed to employ, such as avoiding risk layering, having reasonable geographic and product concentration limits, maintaining tight controls, and closely monitoring lending activity.

FDIC as Receiver of Michigan Heritage Bank v. Cuttle, et al.
Filed August 8, 2011 in the U.S. District Court for the Eastern District of Michigan

The complaint was brought solely against Cuttle, the bank's Senior Loan Officer, Chairman of the Senior Loan Committee ("SLC"), and Chairman of the Commercial Loan Committee. He was not a director of the bank. The complaint alleged simple and gross negligence as well as breach of fiduciary duty. The bank failed with $186 million in assets at a cost of $71.3 million to the DIF.

FDIC as Receiver of IndyMac Bank v. Van Dellen, et al.
Filed July 2, 2010 in the U.S. District Court for the Central District of California

The complaint was brought against four officers that were also members of loan committees but were not directors. This was one of the first complaints filed and the longest complaint with over 60 counts of negligence, waste, fraud, and breach of fiduciary duties. The FDIC sought to recover losses of over $500 million from the loss loans cited in the complaint. The bank failed with $32 billion in assets at an estimated cost to the DIF of between $4 and $8 billion.

FDIC as Receiver for Benchmark Bank v. Samuelson
Filed October 2, 2012 in the U.S. District Court for the
Northern District of Illinois

The complaint was brought against inside and outside directors and officers. The directors named as defendants were all members of the Directors' Loan Committee (DLC). The complaint alleged ordinary and gross negligence against all defendants. The FDIC sought to recover at least $13.3 million in damages, the same amount of the aggregate losses attributed to the loss loans. The bank's failure led to an estimated loss of $64 million to the DIF. The bank had assets of approximately $170 million at the time of failure.

The FDIC claimed that because ADC/CRE lending is a specialized field, officers and directors should have had experience in such lending areas. The complaint claimed the defendants failed to analyze loans proposed to them and approved large loans without "sufficiently informing themselves and considering information necessary to make independent business decisions." The FDIC noted the bank lacked the necessary limits and controls to manage the large ADC/CRE loans.

Additional problems the FDIC cited with the ADC/CRE lending are were that the origination and loan administration functions were not properly segregated to allow for internal control and monitoring. Directors allegedly did not review the bank's own policies before approving loans that had multiple internal and general safety and soundness violations. Moreover, ADC concentration exceeded the bank's internal policy and regulatory guidance.

The 11 loss loans were approved despite the bank not having appropriate capital necessary to make the loans. Therefore, the bank was "forced to enter into participation agreements, under which another financial institution or institutions would buy portions of the loans in order for the bank to remain within its lending limit."

Further, the FDIC noted the bank's lending policy had material deficiencies and the defendants were warned by regulators about the issues. For example, the bank's policy listed the LTV ratio for construction loans could be 80% but regulators guidelines established a maximum 75% LTV ratio. "The policy also failed to require key underwriting data for ADC/CRE loans, such as analyses of the sales absorption period and borrower debt-service ratio."

The complaint claimed there were a number of underwriting issues with the loss loans including outdated collateral appraisals, stale financials, and insufficient credit analysis.

FDIC as Receiver of United American Bank v. Thompson
Filed October 17, 2012 in the U.S. District Court for the Northern District of Georgia

The complaint was brought against inside and outside directors and officers. The directors named as defendants were all members of the bank's Loan Committee (LC). The complaint alleged ordinary and gross negligence against all defendants. The FDIC sought to recover at least $7.3 million in damages, an amount associated with the aggregate losses attributed to the loss loans. The bank's failure led to an estimated loss of $44 million to the DIF. The bank had assets of approximately $111 million at the time of failure.

The complaint alleges, generally, that bank directors were irresponsible in taking unnecessary risks with bank loan portfolios, allowing a high concentration of ADC/CRE loans, and disregarding regulators' warnings regarding underwriting standards and lending activities. The agency also took issue with the bank buying participations without properly analyzing the risks associated with the participations and accepting outdated or inadequate underwriting standards from the other institutions.

Reckless growth strategy was a primary issue cited by the FDIC. The defendants "caused the bank to pursue an aggressive loan growth strategy focused on CRE loans, specifically ADC loans and loan participations." Thus, the defendants substantially deviated from the bank's original business plan. ADC/CRE loans accounted for 642% of the bank's Tier 1 capital. The FDIC claimed that by over-concentrating "the bank's loan portfolio in CRE and ADC loans, the defendants also effectively 'turned a blind eye' to AUB's Loan Policy and prudent underwriting standards."

The complaint claimed that the defendants knew that the economy was slowing. "Despite receiving information showing a slowing of housing sales and peaking of home prices by early 2006, defendants continued to approve high risk and speculative ADC and CRE loans, including the transactions which resulted in the damages."

Regulators repeatedly warned defendants about loan concentrations and underwriting deficiencies with purchased loan participations. The defendants decided to purchase participations despite being "repeatedly warned regarding the extent of those participation loans and the lack of adequate risk management controls."

The complaint alleged that the defendants failed to hire a a qualified chief lending officer to monitor the lending process and put proper oversight measures into place to analyze ADC/CRE loans. Regulators directed the bank to hire qualified staff to address underwriting and risk issues.

The defendants repeatedly disregarded the bank's loan policy and approved loans and loan participations involving borrowers who were not creditworthy and projects that provided insufficient collateral for repayment. Moreover, the defendants repeatedly engaged in a pattern and practice of approving loans and loan purchases that: 1) violated the bank's loan policy; 2) evidenced systematic deficiencies in the credit underwriting, approval, and administration process; and 3) violated sound and prudent banking practices outlined in regulatory guidance.

APPENDIX I

BANK FAILURE STUDIES

LESSONS TO BE LEARNED

There have been a number of <u>post mortems</u> on bank failures. There was a bumper crop following the rash of bank and thrift failures in the late 1980's and early 1990's (the "S&L crisis"). For bank failures since 2009, there have been numerous Material Loss Reviews conducted by the Inspectors General of the FDIC, Federal Reserve, and Department of Treasury.

The studies conducted on the reasons for the bank and thrift failures during and after the S&L crisis can be of help to bank directors. Bank directors are often the means by which a potentially failing bank is turned around before it fails. Effective bank directors can identify the signs of a bank at risk early on, and thereby have time to take corrective action. Learning the characteristics of a failed bank can be helpful. It gives the bank director insight into the causes of bank failures, and what to look for in their institutions at an early stage.

An essential tool as an early warning system for bank boards of directors is the use of red flags. See OCC's "<u>Detecting Red Flags in Board Reports – A Guide for Directors</u>" (February 2004). <u>http://www.occ.treas.gov/publications/publications-by-type/other-publications-reports/rf_book.pdf.</u>

Following the S&L crisis, the Comptroller of the Currency adopted a "Canary System" for its examiners to use to determine at an early stage whether a bank was in danger of failing. It was aptly named because it is the canary that is placed in coal mines to measure, before it is too late, whether there is any lethal gas in the air that will endanger the coal miner. One of the resources listed below is the OCC's "An Examiner's Guide to Problem Bank Identification, Rehabilitation and Resolution". While it is designed for use by national bank examiners, it is also a very valuable resource for bank boards of directors and bank management to help them identify problems early.

Studies on bank and S&L failures during the S&L crisis

Here are some of the studies that evaluated the bank and S&L failures of the late 1980's and early 1990's:

1. The Changing Business of Banking: A Study of Failed Banks from 1987 to 1992. Congressional Budget Office, Washington, D.C. 1994. Prepared at the request of the Senate Banking Committee, the study examined the major factors contributing to bank failures during the period outlined and discussed the extraordinary resolution costs that resulted.
   www.cbo.gov/showdoc.cfm?index=4915&sequence=0.

2. History of the Eighties: Lessons for the Future, FDIC, Washington, D.C. 1998.
   www.fdic.gov/bank/histroical/history/vol1.html

3. Origins and Causes of the S&L Debacle: A Blueprint for Reform, National Commission on Financial Institution Reform, Recovery, and Enforcement, GPO, Washington, D.C. July 1993.

4. Bank Failure: An Evaluation of the Factors Contributing to the Failure of National Banks, Office of the Comptroller of the Currency, Washington, D.C. 1988.
   www.occ.treas.gov/bankfailure.pdf

5. An Examiner's Guide to Problem Bank Identification, Rehabilitation, and Resolution, OCC, Washington, D.C. January 2001. www.occ.treas.gov/prbbnkgd.pdf

6. Compendium Report, Safety, Soundness, and Accessibility of Financial Services: Summary of Treasury OIG's Material Loss Reviews of Failed National Banks and Thrift Institutions

between 1993 and 2002, Office of Inspector General, Department of Treasury, OIG-CA-04-004.
www.ustreas.gov/offices/inspector-general/evaluation-reports/ca04004.pdf

7. Bank Failure Report, An Evaluation of the Factors Contributing to the Failure of National Banks, Office of the Comptroller of the Currency, June 1988.
occ.gov/publications/publications-by-type/other-publications-reports/pub-other-bank-failure.pdf

Other bank failure studies

1. Report of the Board of Banking Supervision (Bank of England) Inquiry into the Circumstances of the Collapse of Barings, July 17, 1995.
www.numa.com/ref/barings/bar00.htm

2. Trends in FDIC Professional Liability Litigation, Insights and Projections Based on the FDIC's First 27 Suits, NERA Economic Consulting, May 31, 2012.
www.nera.com/nera-files/PUB_FDIC_Trends_0512.pdf

3. Characteristics of FDIC Lawsuits against Directors and Officers of Failed Financial Institutions, Cornerstone Research, May 2012.
www.cornerstone.com/fdic_lawsuits_against_directors_and_officers/

4. Trepp Bank Failure Reports, Trepp, LLC.
www.trepp.com/category/research/bank-failure-report/

Material Loss Reviews

Federal law requires the study of certain bank failures by the Inspector General having jurisdiction over the failed bank. Prior to the enactment of the Dodd-Frank Act, Inspectors General were required to review the causes of an individual bank failure if the failure caused at least $25 million in losses to the Deposit Insurance Fund. Dodd-Frank generally limits such required reviews to those involving losses of at least $200 million if the losses occurred in 2010 or 2011, and at least $150 million from 2012 on.

Listed below is a link to each Inspector General website that will allow the reader to review all of the Material Loss Reviews.

Federal Reserve, Office of Inspector General
www.federalreserve.gov/oig/oig_rpt_2012.htm

Federal Deposit Insurance Corporation, Office of Inspector General
http://www.fdicoig.gov/mlr.shtml

Office of the Comptroller of the Currency, Office of the Inspector General
www.treasury.gov/about/organizational-structure/ig/Pages/audit_reports_index.aspx

The American Association of Bank Directors has published a report entitled "What's Wrong with Material Loss Reviews" which concludes that the methodology utilized by the Inspectors General is flawed, leading to flawed conclusions, and that the federal banking agencies (particularly the FDIC as receiver of failed banks reviewing MLRs to help determine whether to sue directors and officers) should not rely on the findings of the Material Loss Reviews for that reason.

APPENDIX II

FDIC Law, Regulations, Related Acts

5000 - Statements of Policy

Statement Concerning the Responsibilities of Bank Directors and Officers

The Federal Deposit Insurance Corporation is issuing this statement in response to concerns expressed by representatives of the banking industry and others regarding civil damage litigation risks to directors and officers of federally insured banks.

Duties of Directors and Officers

Service as a director or officer of a federally insured bank represents an important business assignment that carries with it commensurate duties and responsibilities.[1]

Banks need to be able to attract and to retain experienced and conscientious directors and officers. When an institution becomes troubled, it is especially important that it have the benefit of the advice and direction of people whose experience and talents enable them to exercise sound and prudent judgment.

Directors and officers of banks have obligations to discharge duties owed to their institution and to the shareholders and creditors of their institutions, and to comply with federal and state statutes, rules and regulations. Similar to the responsibilities owed by directors and officers of all business corporations, these duties include the duties of loyalty and care.

The duty of loyalty requires directors and officers to administer the affairs of the bank with candor, personal honesty and integrity. They are prohibited from advancing their own personal or business interests, or those of others, at the expense of the bank.

The duty of care requires directors and officers to act as prudent and diligent business persons in conducting the affairs of the bank.

This means that directors are responsible for selecting, monitoring, and evaluating competent management; establishing business strategies and policies; monitoring and assessing the progress of business operations; establishing and monitoring adherence to policies and procedures required by statute, regulation, and principles of safety and soundness; and for making business decisions on the basis of fully informed and meaningful deliberation.

Officers are responsible for running the day to day operations of the institution in compliance with applicable laws, rules, regulations and the principles of safety and soundness. This responsibility includes implementing appropriate policies and business objectives.

Directors must require and management must provide the directors with timely and ample information to discharge board responsibilities. Directors also are responsible for requiring management to respond promptly to supervisory criticism. Open and honest communication between the board and management of the bank and the regulators is extremely important.

The FDIC will not bring civil suits against directors and officers who fulfill their responsibilities, including the duties of loyalty and care, and who make reasonable business judgments on a fully informed basis and after proper deliberation.

Procedures Followed to Institute Civil Lawsuits

Lawsuits brought by the FDIC against former directors and officers of failed banks are instituted on the basis of detailed investigations conducted by the FDIC. Suits are not brought lightly or in haste.

The filing of such lawsuits is authorized only after a rigorous review of the factual circumstances surrounding the failure of the bank. In addition to review by senior FDIC supervisory and legal staff, all lawsuits against former directors and officers require final approval by the FDIC Board of Directors or designee.

In most cases, the FDIC attempts to alert proposed defendants in advance of filing lawsuits in order to permit them to respond to proposed charges informally and to discuss the prospect of prefiling disposition or settlement of the proposed claims.

The FDIC brings suits only where they are believed to be sound on the merits and likely to be cost effective. On that basis, where investigations have been completed, the FDIC has brought suit (or settled claims) against former directors and officers with respect to 24% of the banks that have failed since 1985.

Nature of Suits Filed

The FDIC's lawsuits are premised on the established legal principles that govern the conduct of directors and officers. Lawsuits against former directors and officers of failed banks result from a demonstrated failure to satisfy the duties of loyalty and care. Most suits involve evidence falling into at least one of the following categories:

• Cases where the director or officer engaged in dishonest conduct or approved or condoned abusive transactions with insiders.

• Cases where a director or officer was responsible for the failure of an institution to adhere to applicable laws and regulations, its own policies or an agreement with a supervisory authority, or where the director or officer otherwise participated in a safety or soundness violation.

• Cases where directors failed to establish proper underwriting policies and to monitor adherence thereto, or approved loans that they knew or had reason to know were improperly underwritten, or, in the case of outside directors, where the board failed to heed warnings from regulators or professional advisors, or where officers either failed to adhere to such policies or otherwise engaged in improper extensions of credit. Examples of improper underwriting have included lending to a borrower without obtaining adequate financial information, where the collateral was obviously inadequate, or where the borrower clearly lacked the ability to pay.

One factor considered in determining whether to bring an action against a director is the distinction between inside and outside directors. An inside director is generally an officer of the institution, or a member of a control group. An inside director generally has greater knowledge of and direct day to day responsibility for the management of the institution.

By contrast, an outside director usually has no connection to the bank other than his directorship and, perhaps, is a small or nominal shareholder. Outside directors generally do not participate in the conduct of the day to day business operations of the institution. The most common suits brought against outside directors either involve insider abuse or situations where the directors failed to heed warnings from regulators, accountants, attorneys or others that there was a significant problem in the bank which required correction. In the latter instance, if the directors fail to take steps to implement corrective measures, and the problem continued, the directors may be held liable for losses incurred after the warnings were given.

[Source: FDIC Financial Institution Letter (FIL--87--92) dated December 3, 1992]

[1]The regulatory agencies and others have produced guides that provide useful advice on ways directors can meet their duties to their institutions. These include the *Pocket Guide for Directors* (FDIC, 1988), *The Director's Book* (OCC, 1987), and FHLBB, Memorandum No. R 62, reprinted at 52 Fed. Reg. 22,682 (1987). See also *The Director's Guide: The Role and Responsibilities of a Savings Institution Director* (FHLB--SF, 1988).

APPENDIX III

AABD Letter to FDIC

Board Loan Approvals

**AMERICAN
ASSOCIATION
OF BANK DIRECTORS**

National Capital Office

Suite 700
1250 24th Street, NW
Washington, DC 20037
Telephone: (202) 463-4888
Facsimile: (202) 349-8080
www.aabd.org

June 23, 2011

The Honorable Sheila C. Bair
Chairman
Federal Deposit Insurance Corporation
550 17th Street, NW
Washington, DC 20429-9990

Dear Chairman Bair:

AABD recently advised bank directors to stop approving loans other than loans subject to Regulation O or involving certain insider conflicts. There are serious risks of potential personal liability that do not justify directors' involvement in the loan approval process unless the FDIC satisfactorily clarifies their appropriate role and corresponding personal liability. We ask that you direct the FDIC to clarify that role as soon as possible. A copy of my Viewpoint American Banker article dated June 14, 2011 is enclosed.

Large banks' boards and director loan committees commonly do not approve loans unless they are subject to Regulation O or internal insider transaction rules. Boards and director loan committees of community banks do commonly approve loans – often reserving their review and approval for the loans with the greatest amount of potential risk, such as large loans and loans that vary in some respect from loan policy.

Based on our review of FDIC complaints against directors of failed banks, we believe that a director's risk of personal liability is heightened by (i) voting for approval of loans; (ii) approving loans where the board or committee has received a board or committee loan package; or (iii) serving on a director loan committee. We are also aware of the FDIC's recent willingness to use its enforcement powers aggressively against directors of failed and open banks for "reckless lending."

A bank director's logical response to these suits and possible enforcement actions would be to do one of the following:

- Resign from the board
- Decline to serve on a director loan committee
- Decline to review or vote for approval of individual loans
- Only approve loans where there is no risk of repayment

Current federal laws, regulations and regulatory guidance do not require a board or board committee to approve any loans other than loans subject to Regulation O. So a board or board committee may choose simply not to be involved in the loan approval process. Directors may meet their fiduciary duties by adopting sound loan policies, procedures and controls, retaining a qualified CEO, relying reasonably on the CEO in assuring that other officers and employees of the Bank are qualified to do the kind of lending in which the Bank engages, monitoring adherence to loan policy and safe and sound lending practices, and taking steps to identify and correct any deficiencies in the lending process. Controls might include independent loan review and internal loan ratings, internal and outside audit of the lending function, and an independent credit function.

An alternative is for the board or board committee to approve only those loans that have no risk of repayment. Loans fully secured by certificates of deposit or by US bonds or notes could be approved, but unsecured loans or loans secured by real estate or other asset that can vary in value would not be.

AABD has advised its members not to approve loans until the FDIC formally clarifies its expectations and requirements for bank directors who want to be involved in the loan approval process.

We urge the FDIC to address the following questions:

- If a board or board committee decides not to be involved in the loan approval process at all (other than as to Regulation O and insider loan approvals under certain circumstances), what other measures, if any, will the FDIC expect the board or board committee to take in addition to the steps described in the first paragraph on page 2 of this letter?
- If a board or board committee relies on a board loan package in considering whether to approve loans, what should that loan package contain and what standards will the FDIC apply in determining whether a director who votes in favor of the loan is legally responsible for any statements or omissions in the board loan package?
- Does a bank director who serves on a director loan committee have a higher risk of being sued by the FDIC or being subject to an administrative action based on reckless lending than a bank director who does not serve on a director loan committee? If not, why is it that most of the complaints filed so far against directors of failed banks highlight that certain directors served on the director loan committee?

Sincerely,

David Baris
Executive Director

Enclosure

APPENDIX IV

FDIC Response to AABD

Board Loan Approvals

Federal Deposit Insurance Corporation
550 17th Street NW, Washington, D.C. 20429-9990

General Counsel

August 1, 2011

Mr. David Baris
Executive Director
American Association of Bank Directors
National Capital Office
1250 24th Street, N.W., Suite 700
Washington, D.C. 20037

Dear Mr. Baris:

Thank you for your letter of June 23, 2011, to the Chairman. Your letter has been referred to me for a response.

You state in your letter that the American Association of Bank Directors ("AABD") "recently advised [community] bank directors to stop approving loans other than loans subject to Regulation O or involving certain insider conflicts." The basis of this advice is AABD's opinion, as also stated in your letter, that large banks' boards and loan committees commonly do not approve non-insider loans while boards and loan committees of community banks do approve such loans and that community bank directors' potential liability would be reduced if they were to stop approving non-insider loans. Your letter finally makes the somewhat disturbing statement that the AABD has advised its members not to approve loans until the FDIC clarifies its expectations and requirements.

The FDIC has not altered its expectations or requirements for bank directors and those standards have remained unchanged for many years. In short, bank directors owe duties of care and loyalty in fulfilling their responsibilities. The FDIC has only filed complaints against bank directors who failed to adhere to these long-standing standards. Consequently, there is no basis for your contentions that the standards require clarification or that the FDIC is imposing new requirements on bank directors that put them at risk of liability for appropriately performing their responsibilities. Bank directors are a critical component in the effective and efficient management of insured institutions precisely because they provide experience and community engagement that may not be otherwise found in bank management. We certainly do not believe it to be in the public's interest, or in the interest of the banking industry, for you to urge bank directors to avoid applying their experience and judgment to important credit decisions for the institution.

Directors of community banks typically approve larger non-insider loans on the merits either at the board or loan committee level. Given the relatively smaller size of a community bank compared to a money center bank, community bank directors are better able to supervise their smaller bank's lending function in this manner. Also as a result, members of community bank loan committees that are directors are in a better position to take prompt action to remedy observed weaknesses in their bank's lending function. Of course, a community bank, both as a legal and regulatory matter, may delegate loan approval authority below its loan committee if it so chooses, provided that the bank's board of directors amends the bank's loan policy to so provide. In fact, community banks often do delegate loan approval authority, at least for smaller non-insider loans, below the bank's loan committee typically to lower level loan officers. If a bank were to do so for all non-insider loans, its loan committee members, whether directors or officers, would no longer have the responsibility to approve non-insider loans on the merits. While this may not be a best practice from the standpoint of good corporate governance for the reasons noted, it is not legally prohibited.

If authority is delegated to lower level officers in the bank's organization, the board of directors nevertheless would retain its nondelegable duty to supervise the bank's lending function. Directors cannot delegate their ultimate responsibility to supervise the core functions of the bank. Directors of financial institutions, large or small, are responsible for establishing the strategic direction of the bank, including managing risks and supervising management to ensure that strategic goals are met. This requires bank directors to undertake diligent and ongoing review of information concerning the bank's operations and performance, including – specifically with respect to the loan approval function – information and data on credit and other risks, loan concentrations, incentive compensation to make loans, and compliance with loan policies, statutes, and regulations, among other things.

If, however, a bank's board has delegated authority to approve non-insider loans to a loan committee, the loan committee members cannot abdicate their responsibility and instead must review loan files and either approve or refuse extensions of credit in accordance with applicable loan policies and safe and sound underwriting standards. If the committee members fail to do so, they risk legal liability that is very well-established by law. If, as is typically the case, the loan committee relies on loan packages to approve loans, the packages must be sufficiently detailed to enable the committee members to make informed and sound business judgments on the merits of the loans that they are approving or rejecting.

The final point in your letter is that over the past year the FDIC has filed several complaints against community bank directors (and officers in some cases) for breaching their duties as members of the failed bank's loan committee. In these cases, the loan committee members had been delegated the authority to approve the loss loans at issue by their boards of directors, but they breached their duties of care, and in some cases their duties of loyalty, to the bank when they approved loans that violated the bank's loan policy and underwriting standards, among other things, and in some instances that were abusive insider transactions.

I am confident that community bank directors will keep these well-established corporate governance and legal banking principles firmly in mind as they reflect on the AABD's recent advice. Thank you again for your June 23 letter to the Chairman. If you have any questions regarding anything in this letter, please feel free to contact me or Richard J. Osterman, Jr., Deputy General Counsel, at (202) 898-3706.

Sincerely,

Michael Krimminger
General Counsel

ACKNOWLEDGEMENTS

I wish to thank my co-author, Jared Kelly, a recent graduate of Georgetown Law School, who wrote drafts of the Report and provided valuable research and review. I also would like to thank Charles Thayer, Chairman of AABD, Robert Ambler and Jamie Connelly of Womble Carlyle, and Aaron Mahler of BuckleySandler for their substantial contributions to the final report.

David Baris, Executive Director
American Association of Bank Directors

DAVID BARIS

David Baris, Executive Director of the American Association of Bank Directors, founded the AABD in 1989 to represent the interests of individual bank directors in the midst of the past bank crisis.

The AABD provides bank directors with the resources to serve their institutions effectively and in a manner that will minimize risk of personal liability, and represents their interests before federal and state legislative bodies, banking supervisory agencies and judicial bodies.

David Baris is a partner in the Washington, DC office of BuckleySandler LLP. Baris represents financial institutions throughout the United States on securities, corporate, transactional, and regulatory matters. Baris has more than 20 years experience advising financial institutions on mergers and acquisitions; tender offers; securities offerings, including trust-preferred securities; proxy contests; and other management and policy matters.

Before joining BuckleySandler, David Baris was a partner of Kennedy & Baris, LLP that he founded in 1987. Baris brings to his legal practice experience as both a bank regulator and Congressional staffer, serving as Regional Counsel to the Comptroller of the Currency from 1977 to 1983 and Counsel to the Government Operations Committee, U.S. House of Representatives from 1972 to 1974.

Baris was a director of Mutual of Omaha Insurance Co. and United of Omaha Life Insurance Co. from 2000 to 2004, serving on their executive, audit, and investment committees.

AMERICAN ASSOCIATION OF BANK DIRECTORS

Founded in 1989 in the midst of the S&L crisis, the nonprofit American Association of Bank Directors (AABD) is devoted to serving the information, education, and advocacy needs of individual bank and savings institution directors.

Bank regulators expect bank and savings institution boards of directors to make informed decisions and to act independently to supervise their institution. One way for CEOs and their boards of directors to demonstrate that their boards are both informed and independent is through membership in AABD – the only banking trade association in the United States which exclusively serves individual directors rather than their institutions.

Bank directors are overburdened, undercompensated, and under threat of personal liability. AABD advocates changes in banking laws and banking agency regulations, regulatory guidance, examinations, and practices that will allow bank directors to better meet their fiduciary duties without being subject to excessive regulatory burdens and unjustified risk of personal liability.

Advocacy: AABD reviews and responds to legislative and regulatory actions that impact bank directors. The Bank Director Regulatory Burden Study, issued in 2012, is a special report that recommends that the federal banking agencies and the U.S. Congress take steps to reduce the huge regulatory burdens imposed on bank directors.

Education: AABD encourages all bank directors to participate in AABD's bank director certification program, which enables bank directors to obtain basic training on their duties and responsibilities and on oversight of lending, investments, ALCO, risk management, liquidity, audit, compensation and other relevant topics.

Information Resources: AABD acts as a central clearinghouse, identifying important resources for AABD members, from bank regulators, the U.S. Congress, national and state banking associations, banking publications and AABD sponsors. AABD provides analysis of developments affecting bank directors.

Banks whose directors are AABD Premium Members receive a complimentary copy of all AABD special reports and publications.

www.AABD.org

15511594R00067

Made in the USA
Charleston, SC
07 November 2012